JEFFREY PEPPER RODGERS

ROCK TROUBADOURS

STRING LETTER PUBLISHING

Publisher: David A. Lusterman
Editor: Stacey Lynn
Assistant Editor: Matthew Kramer
Production Director: Ellen Richman
Designer: Trpti Vanessa Todd
Production Coordinator: Judy Zimola
Marketing Manager: Jennifer Fujimoto

Cover photographs: Jay Blakesberg
All photographs by Jay Blakesberg except the following: pages 4, 18, and 176, Jack
Vartoogian; pages 10, 26, 28, 32, 46, and 52, Sherry Rayn Barnett; page 71, courtesy
Peter Rowan; pages 114 and 117, Danny Clinch; page 161, Steven Stone; page 181,
Cecilia Van Hollen

Printed in the United States of America.
All rights reserved. This book was produced by String Letter Publishing, Inc.
PO Box 767, San Anselmo, California 94979
(415) 485-6946; www.stringletter.com

Library of Congress Cataloging-in-Publication Data
Rock troubadours/ Jeffrey Pepper Rodgers, editor.
        p. cm. – (Acoustic guitar backstage)
    ISBN 1-890490-37-7
1. Rock musicians–Interviews. 2. Rock music–Writing and publishing.
I. Rodgers, Jeffrey Pepper, 1964- II. Series

ML3534.R6343 2000
781.66'092,2–dc21
[B]   00-049258

STRING LETTER PUBLISHING

Contents

Acknowledgments

Rock Troubadours reflects the efforts of many people; I would like to thank a few in particular.

At most of these interviews, I was accompanied by San Francisco photographer Jay Blakesberg, who has a great eye, works fast, and always delivers the goods. His work appears throughout these pages and speaks for itself.

Acoustic Guitar editors Simone Solondz and Scott Nygaard contributed greatly to the process of translating recorded conversation into readable text, as did Stacey Lynn in the process of translating magazine articles into a book. Thanks also to David Lusterman for putting me in the enviable position of conducting these interviews in the first place.

On the other side of the fence, many publicists and managers worked hard to make these meetings happen and to track down arcane bits of information after the fact—thanks especially to Tracy Mann, Steve Macklam, and Brandon Kessler. I also appreciate Joel Bernstein's sharing of information and insights as I tried to unravel the mysteries of Joni Mitchell's guitar style.

Most of all, I want to thank the artists, who are pestered constantly about interviews, for giving up significant chunks of their precious time at home or on the road.

Jeffrey Pepper Rodgers

Preface

Cradled over the smooth wooden curves, fingertips on steel, eyes closed. Listening. It might be a groove, a particularly sweet chord change, an intriguing phrase, maybe a little twist of melody that just has *something*. The songwriter latches onto it, tries to understand its implications. What does it feel like? Where does it want to go? What sort of a song might grow from this tiny, fragile seed?

This moment of creation—and all the decisions and developments that follow it on the way to becoming a fully realized piece of music—is at the center of all the conversations in this book. Musicians, especially famous ones, are forever asked all sorts of questions about their love lives, their vices, and their battles with each other and with the industry, but they are almost never asked what it is they *do* as musicians—in songwriting, with their instruments, in the rehearsal room, in the recording studio, and on stage. The last thing they expect when a journalist comes to call is questions about their craft and inspirations—aspects of life and music that actually *want* to share.

The artists collected in this book include icons of the '60s and '70s who defined what it means to be a modern troubadour, as well as some of the most compelling voices of the younger generation. Though their sounds and styles vary widely, all share an integrity and independence, a distaste for hype and fashion, and, most of all, an individual voice that shines through every note they sing and play. Conducting these interviews under the aegis of *Acoustic Guitar* magazine has been a dream come true for a musician/writer like me, as has the process of revisiting them for this book. Throughout these pages, I was able to include many revealing exchanges that could not be squeezed into the magazine's limited space, so these conversations have a depth and breadth that they've never had before.

My meetings with these artists occurred over the course of nearly a decade, and there were, naturally, new albums and projects in the air that have since been replaced by newer ones. The sidebars that detail the guitars and gear the musicians were using and why—a major obsession of many artists—are particularly subject to change, since the technology of music making advances so quickly. But ultimately what matters is not the specifics of album titles and model numbers but *how* the artists conceive of their projects and choose their tools. From these snapshots in time, we get a glimpse of the cogs and wheels of their creative processes.

All of these conversations have sent me back to the music of the stellar artists with fresh ears and fresh insights. I hope they do the same for you.

PAUL SIMON

"The first time I heard 'Peggy Sue' I was 12 years old," sings Paul Simon over a bouncy rockabilly strum on *You're the One,* his first album of the '00s. His lighthearted return to that seminal moment in music, and in his personal history, was perhaps a necessary curative after his roller-coaster ride through the late '80s and '90s. First there was the artistic and commercial breakthrough of *Graceland,* followed immediately by harsh accusations of being a musical colonialist and defying the cultural boycott of South Africa. Four years later came another world-music triumph with *The Rhythm of the Saints,* a meditation on the drum beats of Brazil. Then *Capeman,* an ambitious piece of musical theater written with West Indian poet Derek Walcott, consumed Simon for the better part of ten years and helped to introduce some of today's finest Latin musicians to a broader audience, only to disappear two months after its debut on Broadway in 1998. During the '90s, Simon also staged several nostalgic reunions with Art Garfunkel, while on other occasions alienating many fans by belittling his old music that they loved so dearly. On *You're the One* Simon offers a striking blend of African and Latin rhythms with the more traditional troubadour mode of '70s solo albums like *Still Crazy After All These Years,* and who knows what slings and arrows and revelations lie ahead.

This 1993 conversation occurred in conjunction with one of the Simon and Garfunkel reunions, during a period when Simon was engrossed in writing the songs for *Capeman.* In many interviews, artists deliver well-crafted but clearly canned responses to common questions. Not so in this thought-provoking conversation, where Simon spoke with the kind of care and intelligence that has always character- ized his music.

THE SOUNDS OF SIMON

What's most striking about the career of Paul Simon is not so much the diversity of the musical terrain he's covered—which is apparent, often commented on, and truly remarkable—but its overall unity. From the shimmering pop folk of Simon and Garfunkel to a solo career that has reached new peaks in the '70s, '80s, and '90s, Paul Simon's music always sounds just like Paul Simon and no one else. The signature lies in his shy voice, his delicate acoustic fingerstyle playing, and, most of all, in his melodic and lyrical gift. Whether he's writing a folk ballad or fronting a Brazilian drum ensemble, Simon has consistently delivered a level of musical sophistication and sensitivity that few other songwriters have achieved.

In March 1993, Simon reunited with Art Garfunkel for a concert in Los Angeles to benefit the Children's Health Fund, an organization that Simon himself cofounded. Supported by an acoustic set from Neil Young and a few cameos by the Great Flydini (aka Steve Martin), the concert was a warm and wonderful return to the best material of Simon and Garfunkel. Their set spanned "The Boxer," "American Tune," "Sounds of Silence" with Young joining in on electric guitar, and a stunning new guitar arrangement on "Bridge Over Troubled Water," providing both a celebration of the past and a revealing look at how Simon sees this material nearly 30 years later.

The next day, Simon greeted me in his hotel suite and offered the following thoughts on the craft and inspiration behind his songs. With the Garfunkel reunion and a Broadway musical in the works, he is enjoying a renewed focus on the guitar, studying fingerboard harmony with jazz fingerstylist Howard Morgen and composing on the guitar for the first time in years. Simon spoke quietly and carefully, choosing his words and taking his time, illustrating some of his points with a few well-placed chords on the Gurian acoustic guitar that sat next to him on the couch.

I was really struck by a couple of your new arrangements of tunes that you played last night—particularly your beautiful accompaniment part on "Bridge Over Troubled Water."

SIMON I've never played it on guitar before. When we did it in concert, we had Larry Knechtel come and play piano, so I never had to learn it on guitar. And then I've done it [solo] many times, but always with piano. So I had to work out a guitar arrangement.

That was an intricate arrangement to do—and fun. It was a little bit harder to stand with a strap and play it. You really want to sit and get close to the neck and concentrate on playing, which I can't really do if I'm standing, and then if I have to sing a harmony. So I simplified the arrangement that I had worked out, but it is a new guitar arrangement for "Bridge." I was playing it in an E fingering, but I tuned the guitar down a half step to E♭.

As far as I could tell, one of your guitars last night was tuned down a half step, and the other was standard. Is that right?

SIMON Yeah. I had been using one that was tuned up a half step, but I switched and went to the standard and used a capo.

"The Boxer" was a half step down. It was in the key of B. I always play it in C, but Artie sings it in B. "El Condor Pasa" was in E♭ minor, but the fingering was in E minor. "Frank Lloyd Wright," the same thing. Those are the tunes that were down a half step.

"So Long, Frank Lloyd Wright" was also a new arrangement. You did some reharmonizing and chord substitution on that one.

SIMON Yeah, because I don't remember the chords that I wrote. And listening to the record doesn't tell me a whole lot. I mean I'm actually surprised at what it is because it's long ago, and they're interesting changes. It took me a while to figure out the changes. I don't know where they came from, you know? I didn't recognize them when I puzzled them off the record. Usually I can remember.

When you wrote that tune originally, had you been listening to Brazilian music?

SIMON Oh, I'm sure I was. Obviously I was. Probably [Antonio Carlos] Jobim. It was probably when I started listening to Jobim.

How conscious are you of the chord theory behind what you're playing? Are you working the chords out primarily by sound?

SIMON Yeah, of course, by sound, by what sounds the most interesting. But I can think of several possibilities of how to approach it, and then it's, which do you like best? Or, do you want to combine them in some different way? But always by ear. And again, if I were recording these I would be playing probably a little bit differently. I'm simplifying when I'm standing up in front of an audience. I don't want to take too much of my attention to the guitar. I just want the guitar to be a constant, nothing to worry about. I concentrate on blending with Artie and giving him a very secure, safe guitar part. If I make a mistake, he's the one who's stuck out there.

Another new arrangement I really enjoyed was "Cecilia."

SIMON Oh, it has a little West African thing. That's a little instrumental I wrote. I just put it into "Cecilia" because the song was so short, so I needed to do something else. It's just open G, always going back to an open-G drone. Just triads, I-IV-V patterns, but used in a West African style so that the chords don't fall the same as [in American music]. They come on different beats. There's much more use of the V chord, and the IV chord is kind of a relief that you go to occasionally.

It's interesting that you've been working on extended fingerboard harmonies with Howard Morgen, yet your last two records have had such straightforward harmonies. Is there a whole other side of your recent work that will emerge in some other form later?

SIMON Yes. The music that I'm writing now is different. There is a lot more use of nines and major sevens, but I'm playing them mostly in broken triads, broken arpeggios. In what I'm writing now, I am playing the guitar as if it were Artie—as if it were a duet. I'm harmonizing with my vocal lines. I'm just using all the notes in the major scale in the simpler things, and not altering the chords too much past sixes, nines, major sevens, the 11 or the sharp 11.

Are you talking about songs that you're writing for the musical with Derek Walcott?

SIMON Yeah.

So you are writing on guitar again. A couple of years ago you weren't doing that at all.

SIMON Yeah. Well, I'm doing both: I'm writing on guitar for sections of it, and I'm using the techniques that I used on *The Rhythm of the Saints* and *Graceland* for other portions of it, when I want the songs to come from the sound. Those albums were coming mostly from the sound of the [rhythm] tracks; I made up the tracks first and then wrote the songs. And now, I'm using the guitar especially on the ballads; because [the musical] is telling a story, there are a lot of ballads, so that you can hear the words. I haven't really been writing ballads for a long time, because *Graceland* was an almost entirely up-tempo album, and *The Rhythm of the Saints* had a couple of things you might call ballads, but essentially not too many.

I understand that you've had physical problems with your hands.

SIMON Yeah. I have some hand problems and a wrist problem now, too, that's been dogging me.

And these problems have led you away from playing full barre chords?

SIMON I can play them now. When it was really bad, I couldn't do the barre chords. I couldn't bend my finger past this kind of angle [bends first finger at very slight angle]. That's a long time ago, but it never really healed. There was some kind of damage on this first finger. If I play a lot it'll get achy, it'll be stiff. Now there is some wrist problem that I can't figure out. They thought I was going to need some orthoscopic surgery, but maybe I'll get lucky and I won't need it. I had a cortisone shot about a week ago, so I could be sure that I could play.

Returning to the concert last night, I noticed that some of your vocal parts sounded a bit different than on the original recordings.

SIMON Like which ones?

"Homeward Bound."

SIMON "Homeward Bound" was a little different, yeah. But I thought it kept the original character.

You and Artie rarely sing a parallel line: you're always moving from unison to different intervals and back again. How did you start doing that? Did you have a certain model in mind?

SIMON We draw upon different musical sources for different sounds. On the simplest of songs, it's just very much like the Everly Brothers. When it's more complex . . . well, we both understand theory and harmony, and we know what choices are available in building a harmony, so if the natural note that you go to isn't satisfying or you can just tell you can do better, we hunt and peck around until we find [something]. Again, because those songs from that time are so simple—many of them are so simple—the reworking of the harmony kept the simplicity, but it was just touching off nines and sixes and major sevens and then falling back into thirds. With that mix, you don't feel that you're in the middle of a jazz tune, and yet it doesn't sound like a folk recording. It's just more interesting harmonically.

But the harmonies that we're singing now are adding notes to the chords that often weren't on the original recording. Sometimes they are; on a song like "Old Friends," Artie is singing a major nine in the harmony, and that was way back then.

Sometimes you use the change from singing in unison to singing harmony to real dramatic effect. I'm thinking of "Bridge Over Troubled Water," when you come in with the harmony part in the last verse.

SIMON I think that harmony [last night] was the harmony I sang on the original recording. Again, I could have sung more harmony on that, except I had my hands full with playing the guitar part, because I've got to give him an accompaniment that feels as complete as a piano. So I'm trying to find the most interesting voicing of the chords but still make use of that open E string.

In past interviews, you've been fairly critical of your older work. How does it feel to go back and play these songs?

SIMON Well, I change the stuff that I find most irritating. Like "Homeward Bound"—that version last night, I find that a satisfying version. I don't like the record, the original record. So it's a way of going back and reclaiming those songs that were innocent and simple and naive. Without losing [those qualities], I try to lose the stuff that was just really young thinking. There's just no reason to preserve it.

Do you mean young musically or lyrically?

SIMON Both. Well, lyrically, I just don't touch it. It is what it is. But you know, if the music is more mature, then I think the younger lyrics don't feel like anything more than just a very young mind, that's all. If the music behind it acknowledges what the emotion is, I don't think you have to change the lyrics to make it what this age is. I could still be whatever I was when I wrote it—22 or 23. I could still be a 23-year-old narrator singing that song, but as the accompanist I have to be more grown up than that. Otherwise it's just too boring.

I'd like to backtrack for a second to ask about your connection with the British folk scene and guitarists like Martin Carthy, who I understand was the original source of "Scarborough Fair."

SIMON I first went over in 1963, briefly, but I lived in England for most of '64 and '65. The English folk scene was a big influence on my playing. Davey Graham was one of the guys who influenced everybody— he influenced Bert Jansch and John Renbourn, who were probably the leading blues folk players. And Martin Carthy was probably the best player, the most musical of the players. That arrangement of "Scarborough Fair" is sort of how I remembered how he did it. Everybody did "Scarborough Fair," and everybody did "She Moved through the Fair"—those were two really big songs.

There was the Ian Campbell folk group from Manchester, with Dave Swarbrick in it as the fiddle player. Ian Campbell's sons are UB40. That group was really good. Lou Killen was a concertina player who was very good. Ewan MacColl was married to Peggy Seeger, Pete's half sister. He wrote "The First Time Ever I Saw Your Face," which was at that point the great folk love ballad, which then became this huge pop hit.

SELECTED DISCOGRAPHY

SIMON AND GARFUNKEL

The Concert in Central Park, Columbia 45322 (1981).

Bridge Over Troubled Water, Columbia 9914 (1970).

Bookends, Columbia 9529 (1968).

The Graduate, Columbia 3180 (1967).

Parsley, Sage, Rosemary, and Thyme, Columbia 9363 (1967).

Sounds of Silence, Columbia 9269 (1965).

Wednesday Morning, 3 A.M., Columbia 9049 (1964).

But the great guitarists were Davey Graham for a sort of blues-jazz style, and his big disciples would be Bert Jansch and John Renbourn, and Martin Carthy for fingerpicking folk.

In terms of your writing and your guitar playing, what did you absorb from them? Did you get into open tunings then?

SIMON Yeah, but I didn't learn that from Martin Carthy. I learned that from a guy named Sandy Darlington, who was an American living over there, who was playing a lot in D A D G A D tuning. I played a little bit in open tunings, but not too much. That's where I learned to Travis-pick.

In what ways do you think British folk informs the music you're writing now?

SIMON I had a very strong liking for English traditional music. I liked the fiddle sounds, I liked the concertina sounds, those kinds of fourths and fifths harmonies in the vocals. So the real traditional stuff stuck with me. The rest of it, it was really imitating the Bleecker and Macdougal folk scene in New York. It was that kind of mix, the two cultures blending into each other. And the folk scene was just a membrane away from the enormous vitality of the pop scene that was happening, so at a certain point the pop groups—like the Beatles—began to come down to folk clubs and pick up licks or tunes. Some pop groups recorded "Homeward Bound" and "Sound of Silence" and "I Am a Rock" before the Simon and Garfunkel hits. The pop scene was absorbing the folk scene into it. But the folk scene thrived. You went from place to place, you played in these pubs, and maybe a big night would be 150 people—that would be a lot.

So you were performing often?

SIMON Yeah, I performed a lot. That was really the first place that I learned how to perform, because I was working all the time. I learned how to talk to an audience, how to pace a set,

SELECTED DISCOGRAPHY

PAUL SIMON
You're the One, Warner Bros. 47844 (2000).
Songs from Capeman, Warner Bros. 46814 (1997).
Paul Simon's Concert in the Park, Warner Bros. 26737 (1991).
The Rhythm of the Saints, Warner Bros. 26098 (1990).
Graceland, Warner Bros. 25447 (1986).
Hearts and Bones, Warner Bros. 23942 (1983).
One-Trick Pony, Warner Bros. HS3472 (1980).
Still Crazy After All These Years, Warner Bros. 25591 (1975).
Live Rhymin', Warner Bros. 25590 (1974).
There Goes Rhymin' Simon, Warner Bros. 25589 (1973).
Paul Simon, Warner Bros. 25588 (1972).

Rhymin' Simon, 1973.

all of those kinds of skills. So when Simon and Garfunkel became a hit and we went out to perform, we were essentially doing my act from my folk days in England.

Which was solo.

SIMON That was solo, yeah. And there's an album I made over there that has never been released here.

I'd like to fast-forward a little bit to your first post–Simon and Garfunkel album [Paul Simon]. From a guitar standpoint, that album has an explosion of energy. "Peace Like a River," for instance, has a fantastic acoustic part.

SIMON That's the last [record] before my finger got hurt. You can hear how much strength there was—how hard I could pull a string and bend a note. Also, you know, I just don't think there's anybody who records acoustic guitar like Roy Halee [Simon's longtime engineer]. He just knows how to record acoustic guitar.

What do you think is the secret?

SIMON There's no secret to anything, you know. It's just the ears; he has great ears. It's the right mic and the right placement of the mic or mics—it's usually a combination.

One close and one far away?

SIMON Not necessarily close and far away, but two microphones may have distinct characteristics, and he may blend 70 percent of one mic with 30 percent of the other. Of course in those days there was nothing direct, so they were all recorded with a mic in front of the guitar. . . .

My guitar parts are usually a combination of guitars: a six-string and a high-string [a guitar with the bottom four strings tuned an octave higher than standard, like the octave strings on a 12-string]. The high-string adds just a shimmer on top.

Have you been mixing the two for a long time in the studio?

SIMON Always. From *Simon and Garfunkel* through probably every record I've made, I'm playing high-string. On the *Rhythm of the Saints* tour, most of the guitar work I did was on the high-string. I've got three guitarists in the band who are incredible, so what am I going to play, you know? I've got to basically put an acoustic, shimmery top on top of Ray Phiri's picking, or Vincent Nguini's fingerstyle picking, and the high-string has the percussive sound of a six-string but it has all the overtones of a 12-string, except there's no midrange—you're only on the upper strings. I use it all the time.

Do you have one guitar that you keep in high-string tuning?

SIMON I think I do have one like that, but it's no big deal—you just string it up to a high-string.

Guitar has been the basis of a lot of your music, but you've also transcended it in many ways, both through keyboard-based harmonies, as on Still Crazy After All These Years, *and through your recent drum-based albums. Have you done that to get past limitations of the guitar as a songwriting instrument, or to get away from certain progressions that guitar might lead you toward?*

SIMON Yes. I take a much more pianistic approach to the writing, with leading tones and [paying attention to] what the bass is. . . .

It's not always the root in the bass. The bass line moves with a certain logic that dictates how the chords are voiced, as opposed to barre here, barre here, strum there. So for ballads, you can write more interesting changes with that approach on guitar.

That's something that I started to do quite a lot in the '70s, when I was studying with Chuck Israels, who is a bass player and composer, so the harmonic approach wasn't a guitaristic approach—it was a bass player's and a composer's thinking. And really not that different from the way Howard thinks as well. And then, of course, the African way is another style. Different styles become available to you if you live through them and play them. You can use elements and find a way of expressing what you want to express, and have it shift from one style to another, and blend the styles. And that blending becomes your voice, your style of playing.

Do you think that learning a lot of chord theory and the like can be a trap, in that if you're aware of all these possibilities, you might feel you have to use them?

SIMON No, I don't think it's a trap. Simple is always a choice.

But some people seem to forget that choice.

SIMON Well, it's not the knowledge that's the trap. How you hear music, what your instinct is, is going to be how you express music. There may be a time when you want to express something that's more complex, and it would be nice to have that available to you if that were the case. And there are times when just the simplest of chords is going to be the most satisfying, and you would want to know that that moment had arrived. So I don't think that knowledge is a trap at all; I think the more technique that you have, the more choices that you have available to you, and the more options you have of expressing yourself. How you express yourself is your nature; it may be very moving, it may be artistic, and it may be banal, but it's not because you had too much knowledge.

You once commented that when you made Graceland *you were trying not to think so much in your writing, and that was part of the reason why you were starting from the rhythms and building up from there.*

SIMON I wonder if I said that.

It's not accurate?

SIMON Well, it's kind of around a point. In the case of *Graceland,* what happened was I began with the sound of the tracks and then wrote the songs. Just like with *The Rhythm of the Saints* I began with the sound of the drums and then wrote the songs. So really, those are like records, and they have more of the quality of records to them than they do of songs. If you took them and stripped them away and went to play them with one guitar, you would find that a lot of those songs were very idiosyncratic, very asymmetrical.

I would cut a track and I'd sing a lyric for the first verse and it would fit fine, and the second verse would be the same amount of bars and the same chord structure, and it wouldn't work. I couldn't figure out why it wouldn't work, and it took me a long time to realize that it was changing—little, subtle changes, and those changes had to be accommodated. It had the feeling of being symmetrical, but it was not symmetrical in the way that our music is symmetrical. It was asymmetrical in an African sort of way, using a theme and variation that was different from the way we have theme and variation. So when you just listened to it, it sounded like it was very simple, but when you actually got in there to try to figure out why something wasn't working, you could see that it was subtly changed in rhythm or accent or a chord for a beat. If you didn't acknowledge that this little thing had happened, then it just wasn't as smooth. And as soon as you did acknowledge it, then it all fit.

Those little differences made the songs asymmetrical in a way that was different from sitting down with a guitar and composing songs. So I didn't think less, I just thought in a way that was not structured the way I had been thinking, but was structured more the way I perceived African music to be structured. I had to give up a certain way of thinking in order to fit with what was happening.

Obviously Graceland *and* The Rhythm of the Saints *were heavily oriented toward drums, but there's a thread in your music all along, a love of the combination of percussion and guitar, with drum sounds beyond the trap set.*

SIMON I've always liked that, yeah. I liked it when I was a kid too. I really liked the Bo Diddley rhythm with the maracas as a big part of the sound. I loved "Iko Iko"—that was just done with percussion. I always liked percussion sounds and hand drums, and maybe that's because there's such a big Latin community in New York, so part of the way you grow up is hearing rhythm with more than just a simple trap set.

I'd like to ask a couple of questions related to lyric writing. Do you perceive a difference between writing in first person and writing in character?

SIMON Well, there's a difference. If you're writing a character that you don't understand, then you shouldn't be writing that character. You're going to be identifying with a character, and you're going to be identifying with something in you; you're trying to find a voice that's not exactly your voice, but you're writing about feelings or emotions that you think you have an insight into.

Take, for instance, the song "The Only Living Boy in New York." I understand that you wrote that song at the time when Artie was going to Mexico to shoot

Catch-22, *but you sing that song to "Tom," and the personal truth behind the song isn't obvious.*

SIMON You know, when we were kids we recorded as Tom and Jerry. . . . He was going off to make a movie, and I was writing a good luck song, really. But since that's so personal in terms of its lyrics, I would hardly expect anyone to get that, a reference that people aren't privy to.

So it has to make some kind of a leap.

SIMON Yeah, I think there has to be something universal for the song to be a really good song. It can't just be that you have to know Paul Simon's private life to get this; there has to be something about it that is available to anybody on some level.

You've written some classic story songs—like "Duncan" and "The Boxer"— that have a particular kind of repetition; the lyrics unfold in a similar way.

SIMON Yeah. They're episodic. Those songs are always fun, you know. If you tell a story, it's always fun. "Graceland" is like that, "Hearts and Bones" is like that. People always like a story song if the story is interesting. I think they're special, those songs—they tend to be good songs, just because of the concentration required to take the story line through to its completion. That means there's going to be a structure to the song. Of course, a song like "You Can Call Me Al" has that element to it and also an abstract element at the same time, so you can combine the forms—episodic and abstract—and make something of it.

Don't the abstract songs have to tell a story in some way, even if it's not in as literal a way?

SIMON They don't necessarily have to tell a story, but they might have to tell a feeling. They have to be evocative; they have to be specific about what they evoke, but it can be shadowy and shapeless and still have some emotional resonance.

On some of the material on Graceland, *your lyrics work in an impressionistic way, with quick flashes of images and scenes.*

SIMON More in *The Rhythm of the Saints* than *Graceland* even. That's a reflection of the tracks, because if you tune in to a drum conversation—a lot of drummers playing and answering each other—there's a call and response going on. And then you lay chords on top of that. To treat that as if you just had a simple, steady beat that wasn't varying, as if this conversation wasn't going on, would be to ignore one of the most interesting things that's happening. So I'm trying to listen in on the drum conversation, and in the same way that you overhear a conversation somewhere that's interesting, and you hear bits of it, you hear some people at another table and they say some sentence that's really intriguing, and then your ear gets pulled over to it [*a horn blares outside the hotel*], and then your ear hears a car horn out the window, and then you're back into the conversation that you're having. . . . The mind is dealing with several aural elements all at once, and sometimes I try to write songs that have that characteristic too.

Maybe this is a stretch, but juxtaposing information in that way seems to be related to the times we're in now, which are different from the times in which you started writing. People are more used to taking in information in small, fast bits.

SIMON I think the attention span is shorter now, and people are used to hearing several things happening at once. Also, so many pieces recall earlier times or pieces of music, and when they do that, if the person has any recollection of the earlier music, then that has an emotional overtone that interacts with the lyrics as well. So the information is coming to you from several, if not many, sources, and that's the way we gather information now. Trying to balance that out in a way that's entertaining and musical requires that you fiddle around with some kind of equation between different sources of information to get the right proportions, so that it delivers something near to the meaning of whatever it is that you're making up. And often you yourself are looking for the meaning of what you're making up; you're on that same journey.

I always like that; I find that very entertaining to be wondering what's going to happen next, as opposed to, "I know what's going to happen; I've got to figure out how to tell it to somebody." That way I get to be the audience to what I'm writing, and if I find it interesting, then I say, "Well, that's OK, I'll keep it, that's interesting," even if I really don't know what it means exactly. That way I get to go along on the ride too, and I get to hear a Paul Simon song without knowing what it is. It's fresh to me.

I feel that there's such a unity to all your music over the years, despite the fact that you've covered such a broad range of styles. Do you see that unity, and if so, what is the basis of it?

WHAT THEY PLAY (1993)

Paul Simon performs with custom-made Yamaha acoustic guitars. The bodies are on the small side, with necks that he calls "very comfortable." These guitars come to him with pickups and volume and tone controls installed, but he's been adding internal mics for amplification. "I'm always trying to find a way to do it better," he says of his amplification setup, "the way everybody who plays acoustic guitar amplified is always trying to find some way of capturing that really pretty acoustic sound."

His favorite acoustic guitar is a Gurian. "In a way, this should be the guitar that I build the microphones in and bring out to play on the stage," he says. "But this is the guitar that I record with, so I don't want to fool with it because I don't want to take a chance that I'll alter the sound."

Simon has a 12-string but doesn't play it anymore, because he'd rather play a six-string and overdub a high-string in the studio. He has some Martins and tends to make them into high-strings, although he adds that "any small, light guitar will be nice in a high-string, will give you a nice, delicate sound."

His guitar collection also includes some Roger Sadowsky electrics, a D'Aquisto archtop, a circa 1952 D'Angelico, and two Velázquez classicals. One of the Velázquez guitars is "just a champion," he says. "But because I'm nervous about my hand, which seems to be OK now but is easily injured, going back from that wide classical neck and the light nylon strings to the steel strings, it just makes me nervous. Unless I really had to get to the nylon for something specific . . . in fact, I think I will go back to that nylon, now that I'm talking about it. It's such a good guitar."

Simon fools around a bit with string gauges, but tends toward lights. He often uses a capo, sometimes in high positions, such as at the seventh fret in the reunion concert with Garfunkel. "That's Artie, that's because of where Artie sings it," Simon says. "I wouldn't normally play above the fifth fret. I really don't like the sound too much above the third fret. When you get up to the seventh fret, it's pretty high, but that's where he wants to do 'Scarborough Fair.'"

Simon occasionally uses fingerpicks on records, such as on a session with Willie Nelson recording "Graceland" and "American Tune." He keeps long fingernails, which he treats with acrylic about once a month to keep them strong. In performance, he often switches between strumming (using his nails) and fingerstyle (using two, three, or four fingers, depending on the song). "That's tricky to do," he says, "because when you strum, your wrist motions tend to be much wider than the control I need for the fingerpicking, and the wrist is in kind of a different position too. So it means that as you come to the end of your strum, you've got to put the control back into where it would be for fingerpicking.

"Needless to say, the more you play the easier all this stuff becomes, and when I'm writing I'm not playing my repertoire. I'm just working on whatever I'm writing, so I'm not getting in a lot of practice on 'Mrs. Robinson,' I can tell you."

SIMON I definitely see it. The basis of it is the earliest rock 'n' roll that I heard. It was a very diverse kind of music that was called rock 'n' roll. I mean it went from the Everly Brothers, with their roots in Appalachian harmonies, and then back to [the 18th-century folk-song collection] *Child Ballads* from England, to Louisiana music, which drew from Caribbean and West African percussion rhythms, to the doo-wop groups that came out of gospel quartets that come from South African choral singing. And I try to reproduce all of those elements of the sounds that I heard when I was a kid, that I loved on records.

The older I get, the more I realize that each period of time, each decade has a character to it that expressed certain ideas and emotions in a certain way. The way people felt and the ideas that were very '60s-ish, they had a certain sound in music. And the same goes with the '50s. And, in fact, the same goes for the '40s. I could hear their certain kind of melodies. Obviously the more recent decades become harder to define, because you need to have the distance to see, "Oh, that melody is very '50s, and it's usually attached to this thought or emotion, and it expresses that thought or emotion very naturally, because that's what that period was about."

So I use [that connection]. I find that it plays on all our subconscious; we associate sounds with times and feelings. I think that our aural recollection is the most powerful; it's more powerful than our visual recollection. I think if you hear a song from a certain time that had meaning to you, it's going to have more emotional wallop than if you see a photo or a movie from the same period, even though they're both something that people get moved about and feel nostalgic about.

So I see [my music] as a unity, and I see that unity being the early roots of rock 'n' roll, white and black: Johnny Cash to Hank Williams to the Everlys to Fats Domino and Professor Longhair and Jimmy Clanton and Clifton Chenier, zydeco to accordion music from South Africa to Delta blues up to Chicago. . . . Each of the sources that became developed in those earlier days, you could identify the real culture that they came from, and now the cultures are so diluted that it's very hard to hear what they are. And especially as the instruments were replaced by machines or samples, it further homogenized the culture and gave us this big, mass MTV culture—which has its own characteristic, and one day people will use that and it will be evocative of this time.

But my writing comes from what I heard in the '50s and '60s and not much past that. In terms of sounds, that's all the information I need. I could be investigating those sounds for the rest of my life and still find it musically satisfying.

JAMES TAYLOR

Compared to the other artists in this book, James Taylor is more a miner than an explorer: from his worldly-wise debut in 1968 to his latest creations, Taylor's songs have always come from the same deep, soulful vein. In the winter of 1991, when this conversation took place, Taylor had just released the lovely, wistful *New Moon Shine,* and his music continued to shine throughout the decade. In 1993, the double-CD set *James Taylor Live* documented the generosity and polish of his stage show, as his empathetic band ran through a career-spanning set of songs. The backdrop of his next studio effort, *Hourglass* (1997), was a series of personal losses: the deaths of his father, his brother Alex, and his longtime producer and friend Don Grolnick. But characteristically, Taylor turned his experience of mourning into music suffused with warmth and light. In our conversation, Taylor talked about finding ways to make the recording process more personal and informal, and on *Hourglass,* he went one step further, recording almost entirely in his house on Martha's Vineyard over the course of two weeks. The result won Grammy awards not only for Best Pop Album but for Best Engineered Album, and it became his most commercially successful release since *Sweet Baby James*— a particularly sweet victory for a 50-year-old veteran artist in an industry obsessed more than ever with the packaging and hyping of young, new faces.

The '00s kicked off with Taylor's induction into the Rock and Roll Hall of Fame, about which the always self-effacing troubadour had this to say: "I was thrilled to even be considered, let alone selected. . . . It's incredible. I demand a recount."

SHED A LITTLE LIGHT

A voice echoes in the hallway outside an Upper West Side apartment in New York. Instantly familiar, it glides over a melody like a stream over worn stones, bringing to my mind a rush of musical memories from the last 20 years, especially a few long afternoons in the mid-'70s spent working out the chords to "Fire and Rain" and "Sweet Baby James." The door opens and in walks the source of those famous songs, James Taylor—only the singing doesn't come from him, but from his teenage son, Ben, who follows close behind. Father and son carry guitar cases into this apartment that acts as a simple music studio, a few floors up from the family living space. "He plays all the time—he's got the bug," Taylor Sr. says of his son. "He's pretty much eaten everything I've got to offer."

Look out for that boy. The musical legacy he has inherited genetically and by good old father-to-son instruction is one of the richest, deepest, and most pervasive in the land of acoustic guitar. (Having Carly Simon as your mother doesn't hurt either.) It's hard to imagine what the term singer-songwriter might mean today without the music of James Taylor. From the reflective ballads that reach back to his rural North Carolina childhood to his sophisticated pop-folk songs of the '70s, '80s, and '90s, Taylor has melded thoughtful songwriting with distinctive fingerstyle guitar to form a sound that has inspired several generations of musicians. On more than a dozen albums, he has musically and commercially bridged the gap that usually separates the folk and rock/pop worlds, and his broad popularity extends unbroken from the singer-songwriter heyday of the '70s to the current boom.

In the early '90s Taylor is once again on a roll, with a slew of concerts, a performance video, and a Columbia album, *New Moon Shine*, that sounds fresher and more energetic than anything I've heard from him in years. Best of all, *New Moon Shine* brings Taylor's trademark guitar playing up front once again, where it belongs.

One of the aims of the singer-songwriter movement of the last 20 years has been to strip down the barriers between the musician and the audience—to minimize the artifice and showmanship, to communicate emotions in songs as directly and openly as possible. In that respect, it's appropriate that James Taylor in person is so much like the gentle musical voice familiar from his recordings and concerts. Sitting down with his guitar close at hand, Taylor talked with me about the development of his guitar playing and songwriting with an honesty and humility not often found in those with genuine "star" stature.

There's something very at home and comfortable about New Moon Shine. *Does it feel that way to you, and does the title signal any kind of rebirth?*

TAYLOR It does feel at home to me. I'm working with people that I've been working with now for a couple of years. It's the second album that Don Grolnick and I have made with James Farber, and I feel good about our method. And I think that Grolnick has become a lot more focused too. . . . It felt very familiar.

It took a little to get to that point where we were in the studio. There was a sort of misbegotten attempt to get in earlier, then we finally did get in.

During that time you were working on the songs?

TAYLOR Right, and I just didn't have enough material ready. I wanted to go in and just record the stuff with guitar and build tracks around it, but it just doesn't seem to be the way I work. It works for me best to be cutting tracks relatively live, with as many of the musicians as possible who will eventually show up on the track. [On *New Moon Shine*] we didn't do a lot of overdubbing, just solos and some sweetening. It was mostly six or seven players at a time, doing the basic tracks.

I'm intrigued by your past comments about how your songwriting has changed over time from being an emotional overflow of feelings to more of a craft, more studied. What does that change mean for the process of songwriting?

TAYLOR I think that there was more urgency about [songwriting] in the beginning, a real dynamic need to do it, and now I'm used to doing it and do it a lot. I'm required to do it, and a lot of things are competing for my time. And I also don't feel as unfulfilled as I did then—it's not as remedial a process.

Does that change make songwriting more difficult, or does it just take longer?

TAYLOR Both of those things are true, I think.

Do your songs go through a longer revision process now?

TAYLOR Most of the work that I have to concentrate on, that needs some kind of a method or a practice, is the lyrical side of things. The musical side seems to always be easily unconscious.

"Slap Leather" from New Moon Shine *certainly sounds spontaneous—you couldn't have labored over that one too much.*

TAYLOR That one took about as long to write as it did to sing. That was recorded in a home studio in Los Angeles with just guitar and drums, and the whole thing is just live. I had had that lyric floating around for a long time, but I didn't know at the beginning of the session just what it was going to come out like.

What do you think about changes not only in your songwriting craft over the years but also in the general state of the songwriting art?

TAYLOR One thing that's noticeable—not to put too fine a point on it—[is that] songs used to be sold as sheet music and written as lyrics and music for people to reinterpret every time they were played, and it's a relatively recent development that they are written to be recordings. And now, certainly in the case of my songs, they are recorded first and written down as sheet music after the fact.

And different technologies . . . When I started writing songs, I wrote with guitar and that was it. The songs were written to be played on guitar and sung by a single voice. But then, working with the band, you begin to write more anticipating what the band is going to sound like. I think there are other levels of it too. Drum machines and synthesized sounds and tracks that are mechanized and effected very much, sounds that are signal processed—I think that that predicts another kind of music and informs a different kind of songwriting. It's sort of like rap is a natural occurrence given the technology of making music now, the way people can make things sound in the studio.

Different people bring different things to [the songwriting world]. There'll be an influx of African music, or we'll get a dose of Brazilian stuff, or some bright light like Bob Marley will introduce reggae in a big way because that's his vehicle, but he's so brilliant that you have to listen. Globalism . . . bringing in a lot of different kinds of music.

Do your feel as if your music responds to that influx of different kinds of music?

TAYLOR I feel as though I'm influenced by a lot of stuff when I write, but there's that external influence, and then there's the ongoing process of my developing guitar style, which basically determines what's going to come out. There are very few songs that I don't write on guitar. The things that I write on keyboard are even more primitive than the stuff I write on guitar. Some stuff I write a cappella—riding down the road with a tape recorder in an automobile. . . . Writing that way without any accompaniment is interesting; that's a good thing for me to do because it frees me up from the elementary guitar style that I work with.

What are some examples of songs you wrote that way?

TAYLOR "Shed a Little Light" was written without a guitar. "Oh Brother." "Slap Leather."

On those songs the melody has to really stand on its own.

TAYLOR That's right, and it frees you up to do things chordally when it comes time to arrange it that aren't dictated by the guitar style.

You've said that your songs are more centered around chord progressions than around melodies. How conscious are you of the theoretical basis of your chords? Do you work them out by feel, or do you think about chord degrees?

TAYLOR Not necessarily chord degrees, but progressions and tone leading and that sort of stuff. It's not that I'm thinking about them—it's just that I have a very clear and very traditional sense of music [based on] church music, Anglican hymns, Christmas carols, that's basically it. Show tunes to a certain extent.

Some of your progressions draw on almost a jazz vocabulary—not that the songs sound like jazz per se, but they're not quite like folk either.

TAYLOR Yeah, but what would you call Joseph Spence? He's definitely a folk musician because he's not schooled. . . . I think that [he played] Anglican church music too. I was amazed to hear him when I was learning to play guitar. He and Ry Cooder very much influenced me.

My music doesn't sound like jazz to me. There are some simple jazz chords—some 13ths and augmented fifths; I play a lot of major sevenths and plus twos—but really a limited jazz vocabulary, for sure, and also very low on the neck, and usually keeping to the root of the chord in the bass. So it's not jazz, and it's not really folk. It's not really church music either, and it has evolved in the context of popular music. It has been informed a lot by the Beatles, a lot by country music, folk music, and a lot of soul music, black music, that I was exposed to.

What I mean to say is that there's a simple vocabulary of chords that I have, and I also have a four-finger picking style that tends to make things very cyclical. I tend to write songs that establish a kind of chordal cycle, and I'll try to fit a melody and lyric into that. More accurately, hopefully, it's a matter of a melody and a lyric happening within that little wheel.

At what point in the songwriting process are your guitar parts polished into their final form?

TAYLOR They get distilled down while the song is written, and then in the studio, in rehearsal, they get polished down.

Your guitar parts may be somewhat simple, as you say, but they are so identifiable as your sound, and they can be difficult to figure out. I know a lot of people have put many hours in with the pause button trying to pick up those parts.

TAYLOR One of the things that throws people off a lot is that I use a capo— seldom higher than the fourth fret—and in some songs I actually shift capo positions. People will see what key it's in and wonder how that can be done.

Only in a couple of songs do I actually modulate by shifting the capo. In "Your Smiling Face" it happens three times. The song starts in F♯ and then moves up to G♯ and then up to A♯.

David Wilcox told me that one of the lessons he learned from your music is not to make the melody note the root of the chord, but a more interesting note in the chord. Are you conscious of that quality or does it just happen in your music?

TAYLOR I'm sure it just happens.

My range is sort of a low tenor, and I'm most comfortable in D or E. I feel like those are my keys—I don't know exactly what that means, of course, because you can put the melody wherever you want in the inversion of the chord. Miles Davis once said to me, "D is your key, James." He said very little else to me. He was very encouraging to me, actually, by his standards. But at any rate, he was right.

I wish I had a higher voice, because I feel as though the open guitar from low E to high E is an interesting range. It's not arbitrarily chosen; that's where the guitar really sounds good, and it's a nice range to hear things in, too. It's nice to be able to put your voice well up above that, like in a good, honest tenor, so that you can sing in F, say, and really get those notes. It puts you high above [the guitar], and I like music that's really opened up, that has wide, very open inversions. It really implies a lot of the overtones, it's very rich, you don't have to use a lot of stuff, and you sort of suggest a lot of notes.

I think that's why I stay down the neck, because basically I play guitar as an accompanying instrument, and just basically get a wheel rolling and then hop on the thing and try to ride it. It's nice to be up high enough that you're not tangled up in it.

Are you playing mostly in standard tuning and then just moving the capo around?

TAYLOR Yes. Sometimes I use a G tuning, very infrequently, and there are a number of tunes where I drop the E down to a D, but that's about it.

James Taylor and Joni Mitchell at Queens College, New York City, c. 1969.

When you are playing in E, for instance, would you use a capo on the fourth fret and then play open-C fingerings?

TAYLOR I like playing in D so much that to play in E I'm more apt to put a capo on the second fret and to play a D fingering.

Aside from the way your voice feels in different keys, do you think the way a guitar is constructed leads you to a certain key?

TAYLOR To me, it's E, A, and D, or G and C— those are the keys that I play in. A and D are the same for me; they have the same kind of tonal quality to them, and the same with G and C. I'm led there. You see, I haven't made that sort of chromatic leap with the guitar where I can play in any key. I'm an open, standard guitar player with folk, blues, and country roots who likes to play in those keys that give you good access to open notes.

Do your songs come more alive for you when you're performing than when you're in the studio?

TAYLOR It's interesting, you know; if the tour lasts for two months, the rehearsals and the first three weeks of it will be the most rewarding time. Then there comes a point where you are feeling as though you're repeating it. It's such a large show—if it's for an average of 10,000 people a night, and carrying sound and lights and stuff that all need cues, and it's being given in an arena context, then you tend not to change it every night. You tend to want to set it into the form that that tour is going to be, and give them the best that you can every night rather than take a chance on it. If you're playing small clubs you can feel a little bit better about changing it up, but those big places tend to freeze the show. So after about three weeks of having it out, it starts to feel a bit like turning the crank.

Do you ever have a chance to get that smaller-venue feeling?

TAYLOR No, most of the places I play are pretty large. You get that small-venue feeling when you know how good you are but nobody else does. At this stage it feels like more is expected of me. It is less spontaneous now.

Do you have guitars around the house and just pick them up every so often?

TAYLOR I don't. I never really did. I have to clear the time and defend it, or else something else eats it.

Nonmusical things?

TAYLOR Yeah. Other things I'm interested in . . .

It's a funny thing. I think that my musical style developed really in a vacuum. It developed in North Carolina with a lot of time on my hands, empty, open time, and I think that's true of a lot of musicians who develop their own thing. It takes a lot of time to practice, and it takes a certain amount of alienation to want to do that instead of wanting to do social things. It means that you in some way are cut off. So in a way, the people who do that are the ones who are the least adapted to or prone to be social and political and stuff like that. It's always a funny and, I think, jarring thing when you bring these things to market, when it starts to be something that happens in a public context. It's a very iffy transition for a lot of players.

For you?

TAYLOR It certainly has been for me. I had a long love/hate relationship with the business, with the idea of representing it and selling it. I've always had very mixed feelings about it. I'm used to it now. I've probably pretty much sold out by now, or found out exactly how to accommodate it.

And it does eat your music—there's no doubt about it. It's not the point, but it looks like the point, and it's the thing that in an established way is taken most seriously.

"It" meaning . . .

TAYLOR The business side, the marketing side, the aspect of it that is expanding yourself into the world and becoming known, more known than you deserve to be or would ordinarily be, you know what I mean? That part is taken very seriously and gets a lot of attention and a lot of interest. It's validated, and it eats your music—it eats it up.

Do you think there's any way around that?

TAYLOR No, I don't think there is. I think some people accommodate it and do it well, but those are people who are evolved people anyway, who don't tend to sink and who don't tend to get thrown off their axis of rotation by surprises and jolts and big changes like that, people who have a good sense of self. But like I said before, that doesn't tend to be an awful lot of

In concert, 1976.   musicians who are starting off, who want to run and hide.

Do you have any advice for those people?

TAYLOR The good advice is to keep in touch with the source.

The musical inspiration?

TAYLOR Just play your music, and do it for the people who love it for music. In other words, play it in public, play it in private for people who love it, go on the road with it, play it for other musicians, and try to minimize the extent to which you are playing it for someone's marketing scheme, to accommodate somebody's idea of how to sell it and how to move it as a product. That's confusing, and that's not the point. [Music] exists for an emotional reason and not for a commercial one, primarily.

It must take a strong sense of your own identity to stay in touch with that source as you go along.

TAYLOR I think what it means is that you get lost for a while and then hopefully you find your way back. I like Neil Young, you know. He has a T-shirt that says, "This tour is sponsored by nobody." I like his immediate and sort of chemical aversion for advertising and marketing, and he doesn't want to be sponsored. I admire Neil Young's ability to survive and continue to make music for the right reasons, and not to take too seriously—or at all seriously—the marketing side. . . .

Don't get me wrong—I don't think of it as a great evil, I just think of it as an inevitable, confusing thing. People increasingly exist [through their] interface with the great marketplace, but it fools people because it doesn't really exist—it's not really a place. Nobody actually lives in the TV, you know. We live in our communities, we live in our families, but we identify ourselves in terms of these images we see on television. We live in our bodies, but we think we can give 'em the slip [*laughs*].

To me, the songs on New Moon Shine *are filled with the same soul that moved me when I was learning guitar and spending a lot of time with your songs from the* Sweet Baby James *era. Obviously the business side goes on, but so does that source you were talking about.*

TAYLOR I'm glad you think so. Sometimes I worry about it, but I basically think that that's true also. And the way I know is that I still enjoy it; I still feel emotionally connected to it.

SELECTED DISCOGRAPHY

Hourglass, Columbia 67912 (1997).

James Taylor Live, Columbia 47056 (1993).

New Moon Shine, Columbia 46038 (1991).

Never Die Young, Columbia 40851 (1988).

That's Why I'm Here, Columbia 40052 (1985).

Dad Loves His Work, Columbia 37009 (1981).

Flag, Columbia 36058 (1979).

JT, Columbia 34811 (1977).

Greatest Hits, Warner Bros. 2979 (1976).

In the Pocket, Warner Bros. 2912 (1976).

Gorilla, Warner Bros. 2866 (1975).

Walking Man, Warner Bros. 2794 (1974).

One Man Dog, Warner Bros. 2260 (1972).

Mud Slide Slim and the Blue Horizon, Warner Bros. 2561 (1971).

Sweet Baby James, Warner Bros. 1843 (1970).

James Taylor, Capitol 97577 (originally released 1968).

WHAT THEY PLAY (1991)

James Taylor plays three guitars by Minnesota luthier James Olson. Two have an SJ body shape, one with a cutaway (because Taylor likes the sound, not because he plays up high on the neck), one without. One has East Indian rosewood back and sides, a cedar top, and a neck more like a Gibson and a Martin, Taylor says. The third is a dreadnought, which he says he likes a lot, but he adds, "I find as a member of a band that dreadnoughts get in the way of the bass and conflict with the piano. It's nice to have a narrower range of sound, so I like a slightly higher pitched guitar—not tuned up high, but a little thinner body, a little narrower range, so that it's not stomping over all kinds of other things."

He also has a reliable, good-sounding Yamaha and three sizes of guitars by Mark Whitebook: a little saddle guitar, a couple of dreadnoughts, and a steel-string that's more like a classical in size. Taylor says he loves those guitars but finds they're a little too fragile for the rigors of the road. Whitebook is no longer building guitars because of both health and money reasons, Taylor says.

Taylor holds forth on the differences between handmade and factory guitars: Individual luthiers are "not varying the structure of the guitar that much, but they can shave the ribs down where they meet the body of the guitar, because they're doing it by hand, to extremely fine tolerances. They pay close attention to the grain of every piece of wood that goes into it, so they get very strong, reliable, and consistent bracing. They pay a lot of attention to the pieces of wood that go into the top, and they can take it down—really make it thin. They can get away with a much finer finish on it, hand buffed. They're working for your guitar style, what gauge of strings you will put on it, how hard you're going to hammer on the thing, what kind of temperature differences it will go through in its lifetime, what kind of hell you're going to put it through under the lights or sweating all over it, getting it wet, traveling in a cold truck, or whatever. They know these things and they know what the tolerances are. . . . That's what you get when you buy a $2,000 custom-made guitar, and that's what you should be getting."

Taylor's Yamaha has Yamaha electronics for amplification; the Olsons have L.R. Baggs pickups. Taylor does not mic his guitar on stage. He runs the pickup output through a Pendulum preamp, and he says that the preamp's notch filter helps him get the best results from the piezo pickup; he can zero in on and cut the worst-sounding parts of the midrange, then add "crispies" and a little bit of bass.

Even when practicing alone, Taylor sometimes amplifies his guitar and puts effects on it. For songwriting, he says he also enjoys working with a drum machine to set down the rhythm pattern, and he makes demos with additional parts like a synth bass line, a piano part, additional guitar, or vocal harmonies. His New York setup includes a Tascam four-track.

Taylor used to play with strings made by Phil Petillo. Petillo makes great strings, Taylor says, but his travel schedule necessitated finding a standard, widely available brand, and Kaman Adamas light phosphor-bronze strings fit the bill. His guitar tech on the road prefers the strings for their tuning accuracy.

When recording his guitar, Taylor says, "We use two very directional mics, with the heads together and the barrels going off at right angles, and that phase-cancels a lot of the vocal that would otherwise be in those mics." (He usually sings and plays at the same time in the studio.) Taylor likes a little doubling on the guitar part to give it a sense of space, plus a hint of chorusing. He also records the direct feed from the pickup and often puts effects on that rather than on the mic output.

JONI MITCHELL

Of the hundreds of interviews I've done with all sorts of creative, colorful souls, none can quite compare with the fuse-blowing intensity of a three-hour conversation with Joni Mitchell in 1996. I had been pursuing this meeting unsuccessfully for a number of years, not only because of the usual hoops a journalist has to jump through to secure an audience with a star, but also because of Mitchell's long-sour relationship with the press and her deep bitterness about being misunderstood, misrepresented, and underappreciated as an artist. Everything finally fell into place at an auspicious moment: fresh off of a Grammy victory for *Turbulent Indigo* and a lifetime-achievement Century Award from *Billboard,* she was feeling cautiously optimistic about regaining her footing in the music world.

"Interview" isn't quite the word for what happened when we met at a restaurant in Bel Air (chosen because it was one of precious few places in L.A. that would allow her to smoke in an enclosed space);

she had so much she wanted to explain and unload that I felt more like a catalyst than a journalist. At one point, after ten or 15 minutes of nonstop talking, she paused and added with a laugh: "So am I sounding like a complete arrogant asshole or what? It's funny to talk about this stuff. I thank you for the opportunity, for one thing, because I don't usually get to talk about the craft, but in spite of these awards lately, I'm still a little bogged. I'm coming out of a dark ages, in a certain way, so I'm a little, I don't know. . . . I've been compared to so many mediocre things that I'm defensive, I guess that's what you'd have to say, and intense in trying to describe—'Can't you tell the difference between silk and polyester? [*Laughs.*] Well, let me tell you about the fibers—they're quite different.'"

In the years since this conversation, Mitchell has continued to emerge from those dark ages, becoming much more available both to her fans (most notably, touring with Bob Dylan and Van Morrison in 1998 and then solo in 2000) and to the media. Her discography has expanded as well, with *Taming the Tiger* (the album in progress at the time of this interview), the retrospective collections *Hits* and *Misses,* and a set of standards performed with an orchestra, *Both Sides Now.* Meanwhile, the awards and tributes have continued to pile up, including her induction into the Rock and Roll Hall of Fame in 1997.

MY SECRET PLACE

At the heart of the music of Joni Mitchell is a constant sense of surprise and discovery. The melodies and harmonies rarely unfold in ways that our ears, tamed by pop-music conventions, have come to expect. Her guitar doesn't really sound like a guitar: the treble strings become a cool-jazz horn section; the bass snaps out syncopations like a snare drum; the notes ring out in clusters that simply don't come out of a normal six-string. And her voice adds another layer of invention, extending the harmonic implications of the chords and coloring the melody with plainspoken commentary as well as charged poetic imagery.

Even though all these qualities have made Mitchell one of the most revered songwriters of our time, an inspiration for several generations of musicians, the creative processes and impulses behind her music have always been clouded in mystery. A guitarist haunted by Mitchell's playing on an album like *Court and Spark* or *Hejira,* for instance, can't find much help in the music store in exploring that sound; what she plays, from the way she tunes her strings to the way she strokes them with her right hand, is utterly off the chart of how most of us approach the guitar. To date, the only published documentation of her 30-year guitar odyssey is in a handful of single-album songbooks that show the real tunings and chord shapes, although now the Web is disseminating this information more widely. In the view of Joel Bernstein, Mitchell's longtime guitar tech and musical/photographic archivist, precious few players have fully understood her style and followed in her footsteps—in fact, only one, the instrumental pioneer Michael Hedges.

In the wake of her 1996 Grammy for Best Pop Album for *Turbulent Indigo,* which marked the stunning return of her acoustic guitar to center stage, Joni Mitchell met with me in Los Angeles to offer a rare, in-depth view into her craft as a guitarist and composer. To orient myself better in the world of Mitchell's guitar, I also spoke with Joel Bernstein and studied the work of Jim Leahy and the other contributors to the guitar pages of www.jonimitchell.com, which includes an exhaustive list of tunings.

Remarkably, Mitchell herself relies on Bernstein's encyclopedic knowledge of her work; because Mitchell has forged ahead with new tunings throughout her career and rarely plays her past repertoire, Bernstein has at several junctures helped her relearn some of her older songs.

"There's a certain kind of restlessness that not many artists are cursed or blessed with, depending on how you look at it," Mitchell said. "Craving change, craving growth, seeing always room for improvement in your work." In that statement lies the key to her music: seeing it as an ongoing process of invention, rather than a series of discrete and final statements.

LEARNING AND UNLEARNING THE GUITAR

As a child in rural Alberta, Canada, Joni Mitchell went through several instruments on the way to discovering the guitar. First, two young playmates—a classical piano protégé and an opera student—inspired her to play the piano. "I wanted to compose," she recalled. "I started dreaming beautiful music in my head. I studied piano for a year, but the way that piano was taught at that time was that if you weren't a good sight-reader they rapped your knuckles with a ruler. Apparently that was just the way education occurred at that time. But it was unpleasant and basically killed my desire."

She continued, "In my late teens, as some of my friends began to go to college, there sprang up this kind of college student party where people sat

around and sang folk songs. They were becoming politically conscious, and they discovered the Weavers and so on, but no one really played guitar. This renaissance of everybody playing an instrument hadn't really occurred, and the idea of choosing a musical career hadn't occurred to anybody—this is pre-Beatles stuff, you know. So even the idea of wanting to compose when you're eight years old must have seemed ludicrous coming from where I come from. It was misunderstood and suppressed. The only kind of musical education that was encouraged in that community was the classics, the idea of becoming a piano teacher or something.

"At 18 I bought myself a baritone ukulele, basically just to accompany bawdy drinking songs at weenie roasts and college singalongs. I didn't have the money to buy a guitar, and my parents wouldn't buy me a guitar because I had abandoned my piano lessons. They had this opinion that I was a quitter. In six months I could negotiate about six chords or something, so I could play basically anything in one key unless it stretched out harmonically. But it was nothing like the beautiful music I heard in my head and wanted to play on the piano. One had almost nothing to do with the other."

When Mitchell moved to Toronto to go to art school, she connected with the emerging folk scene and—like countless other children of the '60s—with the guitar. "When I was learning to play guitar, I got Pete Seeger's *How to Play Folk-Style Guitar,*" she recalled. "I went straight to the Cotten picking. Your thumb went from [*imitates alternating-bass sound*] the sixth string, fifth string, sixth string, fifth string . . . I couldn't do that, so I ended up playing mostly the sixth string but banging it into the fifth string. So Elizabeth Cotten definitely is an influence; it's me not being able to play like her. If I could have I would have, but good thing I couldn't, because it came out original."

At the same time that she departed from standard folk fingerpicking, Mitchell departed from standard tuning as well (only two of her old songs—"Tin Angel" and "Urge for Going"—are in standard tuning). "In the beginning, I built the repertoire of the open major tunings that the old black blues guys came up with," she said. "It was only three or four. The simplest one is D modal [D A D G B D]; Neil Young uses that a lot. And then open G [D G D G B D], which is all Keith Richards plays in—with the sixth string removed. And open D [D A D F♯ A D]. Then going between them I started to get more 'modern' chords, for lack of a better word." As she began to write songs in the mid-'60s, these tunings became inextricably tied to her composing.

On Mitchell's first three albums, *Joni Mitchell* (1968), *Clouds* (1969), and *Ladies of the Canyon* (1970), conventional open tunings coexist with other tunings that stake out some new territory. "Both Sides Now" (capo II) and "Big Yellow Taxi," for instance, are in open E (E B E G♯ B E—the same as open D but a whole step higher); and "The Circle Game" (capo IV) and "Marcie" are in open G. But it was more adventurous tunings like C G D F C E ("Sistowbell Lane"), with its complex chords created by simple fingerings, that enthralled her and became the foundation of her music from the early '70s on.

"Pure majors are like major colors; they evoke pure well-being," she said. "Anybody's life at this time has pure majors in it, given, but there's an element of tragedy. No matter what your disposition is, we are air breathers, and the rain forests coming down at the rate they are . . . there's just so much insanity afoot. We live in a dissonant world. Hawaiian [music], in the pure major—in paradise, that makes sense. But it doesn't make sense to make music in such a dissonant world that does not contain some dissonances."

The word *dissonances* implies harsh or jarring sounds, but in fact, the "modern chords" that Mitchell found in alternate tunings have an overall softness to them, with consonances and dissonances gently playing off each other. It's difficult to put a label on these sounds, but Mitchell is emphatic about one thing: they're a long way from folk music. "It's closer to Debussy and to classical composition, and it has its own harmonic movement that doesn't belong to any camp," she said. "It's not jazz, like people like to think. It has in common with jazz that the harmony is very wide, but there are laws to jazz chordal movement, and this is outside those laws for the most part."

Initially, Mitchell said, her harmonies sounded strange and troubling to some people, but gradually pop listeners became accustomed to a broader vocabulary of chords. In explaining the power of harmonies to disturb, she cited an example from *Turbulent Indigo.* "There's a change that I use on the first song ['Sunny Sunday'] that was forbidden for centuries. It's called the Devil's interval. When the church controlled music, as it did for many years, it forbade this because it evoked doubt. Well, I'm sure you have your doubts in these times and so do I, and it's the perfect chord change for this thing." She sang the line, "That one little victory, that's all she needs," explaining that the interval in question is the one from *all* to *she.* "There's nothing devilish about it, except that in church music, it throws you back on yourself. It is the emotional equivalent of a *but.* Yes, but. They don't want any *buts* in Catholic religious music. It's 'yea, yea, yea,' with a little bit of sorrow penetrating it—the minor, but that's it."

So how does Mitchell discover the tunings and fingerings that create these expansive harmonies? Here's how she described the process: "You're twiddling and you find the tuning. Now the left hand has to learn where the chords are, because it's a whole new ballpark, right? So you're groping around, looking for where the chords are, using very simple shapes. Put it in a tuning and you've got four chords immediately—open, barre five, barre seven, and your higher octave, like half fingering on the 12th. Then you've got to find where your minors are and where the interesting colors are—that's the exciting part.

"Sometimes I'll tune to some piece of music and find [an open tuning] that way, sometimes I just find one going from one to another, and sometimes I'll tune to the environment. Like 'The Magdalene Laundries' [from *Turbulent Indigo;* the tuning is B F♯ B E A E]: I tuned to the day in a certain place, taking the pitch of bird songs and the general frequency sitting on a rock in that landscape."

Mitchell likens her use of continually changing tunings to sitting down at a typewriter on which the letters are rearranged each day. It's inevitable that you get lost and type some gibberish, and those mistakes are actually the main reason to use this system in the first place. "If you're only working off what you know, then you can't grow," she said. "It's only through error that discovery is made, and in order to discover you have to set up some sort of situation with a random element, a strange attractor, using contemporary physics terms. The more I can surprise myself, the more I'll stay in this business, and the twiddling of the notes is one way to keep the pilgrimage going. You're constantly pulling the rug out from under yourself, so you don't get a chance to settle into any kind of formula."

To date, Mitchell said that she has used more than 50 tunings. This number is so extraordinarily high in part because her tunings have lowered steadily over the years, so some tunings recur at several pitches. Generally speaking, her tunings started at a base of open E and dropped to D and then to C, and these days some even plummet to B or A in the bass. This evolution reflects the steady lowering of her voice since the '60s, a likely consequence of heavy smoking.

"I can't sing in the key of E anymore," she said. "I used to be a pseudo-soprano; now I think I'm an alto. I listened to a CBC compilation that cut together interviews from my 20s with recent interviews, and you'd never know it was the same person. I mean, what a girlie little voice! The smoking has really developed the low end of my voice—quite nicely, as a matter of fact—but it has robbed me a little of the high end."

When Mitchell performs an older song today, she typically uses a lowered version of the original tuning. "Big Yellow Taxi," originally in open E, is now played in a low version of open C (C G C E G C, which is the same as open E dropped two whole steps). She recorded "Cherokee Louise" on *Night Ride Home* with the tuning D A E F♯ A D; when she performed it on the Canadian TV show *Much Music* in 1995, she played it in C G D E G C—a whole step lower. In some cases, the same relative tuning pops up in different registers for different songs: "Cool Water" *(Chalk Mark in a Rain Storm)* and "Slouching towards Bethlehem" *(Night Ride Home)* are in D A E G A D; a half step down, C♯ G♯ D♯ F♯ G♯ C♯, is the tuning for "My Secret Place" *(Chalk Mark)*; another half step lower, C G D F G C, is the tuning for "Night Ride Home"; and a half step below that, B F♯ C♯ E F♯ B, is the tuning for "Hejira."

These connections allow Mitchell, in some cases, to carry fingerings from one tuning to another and find a measure of consistency, but each tuning has its own little universe of sounds and possibilities. "You never really can begin to learn the neck like a standard player, linearly and orderly," she said. "You have to think in a different way, in moving blocks. Within the context of moving blocks, there are certain things that you'll try from tuning to tuning that will apply."

Mitchell has come up with a way to categorize her tunings into families, based on the number of half steps between the notes of adjacent strings. "Standard tuning's numerical system is 5 5 5 4 5, with the knowledge that your bass string is E, right?" she said. "Most of my tunings at this point are 7 5 or 7 7, where the 5 5 on the bottom [usually] is. The 7 7 and the 7 5 family tunings are where I started from." Examples of 7 5 tunings are D A D G B D (used for "Free Man in Paris," *Court and Spark*) and C G C E G C ("Amelia," *Hejira*): in both cases, the fifth string is tuned to the seventh fret of the sixth string, and the fourth string is tuned to the fifth fret of the fifth string. Similarly, examples of 7 7 tunings are C G D G B D ("Cold Blue Steel and Sweet Fire," *For the Roses*) and C♯ G♯ D♯ E♯ G♯ C♯ ("Sunny Sunday," *Turbulent Indigo*): the intervals between the sixth and fifth strings, and the fifth and fourth strings, are seven frets.

Mitchell continued, "However, the dreaded 7 9 family—I have about seven songs in 7 9 tunings—are in total conflict with the 7 5 and the 7 7 families. They're just outlaws. They're guaranteed bass clams [*laughs*], 'cause the thumb gets used to going automatically into these shapes, and it has to make this slight adaptation." Mitchell's 7 9 songs include "Borderline," "Turbulent Indigo," and "How Do You Stop" (*Turbulent Indigo*), all of which are in the tuning B F♯ D♯ D♯ F♯ B.

Just to confuse the fingers further, Mitchell also has some renegade

JONI MITCHELL

tunings in which she's written only one song. Consider the tuning for "Black Crow," from *Hejira*: B♭ B♭ D♭ F A♭ B♭, with the fifth and sixth strings an octave apart. By Mitchell's numerical system, this would be a 12 3 tuning—a very long way from 7 7 or 7 5, and a thousand miles from standard tuning.

An interesting tuning can be fertile ground for writing a song, but—as a whole pile of eminently forgettable new-age guitar CDs illustrate—it's how you work the tuning with your hands and compositional sense that counts. Throughout her music, Mitchell makes the most of the freedom that open tunings allow in traveling around the neck. One of her stylistic signatures is the way she juxtaposes notes fretted high on the neck against ringing open strings. This is a great way to extend the range of the accompaniment, as you can hear on songs like "Chelsea Morning" (*Clouds*, open E), in which she plays a riff up high on the top two strings that dances over the open bass strings, followed by a fretted bass part that moves below the open treble strings.

In Mitchell's later songs, with their more radical tunings, the ringing open strings take on a different sort of drone quality—she uses them between chords as a sort of connecting thread in the harmony. "It's like a wash," she said. "In painting, if I start a canvas now, to get rid of the vertigo of the blank page, I cover the whole thing in olive green, then start working the color into it. So every color is permeated with that green. It doesn't really green the colors out but it antiques them, burnishes them. The drones kind of burnish the chord in the same way. That color remains as a wash. These other colors then drop in, but always against that wash."

Upper melodies, moving bass lines, drone strings: all these components of Mitchell's guitar style are rooted in her conception of the guitar as a multivoiced instrument. "When I'm playing the guitar," she said, "I hear it as an orchestra: the top three strings being my horn section, the bottom three being cello, viola—the bass being indicated but not rooted yet." The orchestral effect is particularly vivid on a song like "Just Like This Train" (*Court and Spark*), with its "muted trumpet parts" and independent lines on the top, middle, and bottom strings.

Mitchell compares the right-hand technique that maintains these separate voices to harp playing, with its fluid movement over the strings. Here's how Joel Bernstein described the evolution of that style: "Her first album has some very fine, detailed fingerpicking—note for note, there are very specific figures. As time goes on, she gets into more of a strumming thing until it becomes more like a brush stroke—it's a real expressive rhythmic thing. Her early stuff doesn't really swing, there's not jazz stuff going on in it, and she's not implying a rhythm section as much, whereas now she obviously has a lot going on in the right hand. It's at the same time simpler and deeper."

Ever since the *Blue* album, percussive sounds have been central to Mitchell's guitar style—a clear influence on all sorts of tapping and slapping contemporary players. Mitchell's inspiration for these sounds came from a surprising place: an encounter with a dulcimer maker at the 1969 Big Sur Festival. "I had never seen one played," she said. "Traditionally it's picked with a quill, and it's a very delicate thing that sits across your knee. The only instrument I had ever had across my knee was a bongo drum, so when I started to play the dulcimer I beat it. I just slapped it with my hands. Anyway I bought it, and I took off to Europe carrying a flute and this dulcimer because it was very light for backpacking around Europe. I wrote most of *Blue* on it."

For about a year, Mitchell played the dulcimer and didn't have a guitar on hand. "I was craving a guitar so badly in Greece," she said. "The junta had repressed the population at that time. They were not allowed public meetings; they were not allowed any kind of boisterous or colorful expression. The military was sitting on their souls, and even the poets had to move around. We found this floating poets' gathering place, and there was an apple crate of a guitar there that people played. I bought it off them for 50 bucks and sat in the Athens underground with transvestites and, you know, the underbelly running around—and it was like a romance. It was a terrible guitar, but I hadn't played one for so long, and I began slapping it because I had been slapping this dulcimer. That's when I noticed that my style had changed.

"I thought that slap came purely from the dulcimer until I saw a television show [recently] that I did the day after Woodstock, where Crosby, Nash, and Stills showed up. Stephen slapped his guitar, which is a kind of flamenco way of playing it, so I would have to cite Stephen Stills also as an influence in that department. But it was latent and not conscious. It wasn't like I studied him and tried to play like him, but I admired the way he played. That's the way I grow, by admiration and not by intellect. Anytime I admire something, something expands, and somewhere down the road that admiration works on me as an influence."

A NEW BREED OF POET

Where Mitchell's songs really come to life is in the way the shifting textures of her guitar meet the melody and lyric and the chorus of supporting voices and instruments. In discussing her slant on the lyric craft, Mitchell recalled her days as an art student in Toronto, when she was performing music on the side—mainly the English folk repertoire—but had not yet started writing songs. "I didn't really begin to write songs until I crossed the border into the States in 1965," she said. "I had always written poetry, mostly because I had to on assignment. But I hated poetry in school; it always seemed shallow and contrived and insincere to me. All of the great poets seemed to be playing around with sonics and linguistics, but they were so afraid to express themselves without surrounding it in poetic legalese. Whenever they got sensitive, I don't know, I just didn't buy it."

Outside of school, Mitchell still found herself writing poems when a strong emotion hit her, such as when a friend committed suicide. But it wasn't until she heard Bob Dylan's "Positively Fourth Street" that she finally began to understand how to tap the power of this private poetry in a song. She recalled, "When I heard that—'You've got a lot of nerve to say you are my friend'—I thought, now *that's* poetry; now we're talking. That direct, confronting speech, commingled with imagery, was what was lacking for me." Later, in the '70s, Mitchell found her ideal of poetry reflected in the words of Friedrich Nietzsche's character Zarathustra, who envisions "a new

breed of poet, a penitent of spirit; they write in their own blood." She added, "I believe to this day that if you are writing that which you know firsthand, it'll have greater vitality than if you're writing from other people's writings or secondhand information."

Thanks in large part to Mitchell's influence, personally based writing became one of the emblems of the singer-songwriter movement that flowered in the '70s and is going strong again. Even today, her 1971 album *Blue* (Reprise) stands as one of the most emotionally naked performances ever captured on tape. The songs are unquestionably written in her own blood, and even though she has progressed through many modes of writing since then—some more obviously autobiographical than others—her personal commitment to the words always shines through.

"I was opened up," she said of her *Blue* period. "As a matter of fact, we had to close the doors and lock them while I recorded that, because I was in a state of mind that in this culture would be called a nervous breakdown. In pockets of the Orient it would be considered a shamanic conversion. It begins with a sense of isolation and of not knowing anything, which is accompanied by a tremendous panic. Then clairvoyant qualities begin to come in, and you and the world become transparent, so if you're approached by a person, all their secrets are not closeted. Like a Gypsy, you get too much of a read on who a person is. It makes you see a lot of ugliness in people that you'd rather not know about, and you lie to yourself and say something nice about them to cover it up. It gets very confusing. In that state of mind I was defenseless as a result, stripped down to a position of absolutely no capability of the normal pretension that people have to survive.

"When the record first came out, I played it for Kris Kristofferson, who said, 'God, Joan, save something of yourself.' He was embarrassed by it. I think generally at first that people were embarrassed by it, that in a certain way it was shocking, especially in the pop arena. People [usually sing], 'I'm bad, I'm bad, I'm great, I'm the greatest.' It's a phony business, and people accept the phoniness of it. It's fluff, it's this week's flavor and it gets thrown out, and it isn't supposed to be anything really more than that."

The experience of *Blue* has not been repeated, she said, but it left her forever changed. "By the time I made the next albums, I had stabilized psychologically, I would say, to a degree where, like we all do, I had some defenses. But that descent cracked me wide open, and I remain wide open to this day. I don't want to develop too many defenses. I'm a kind of experiment, a freak of nature. I'm going through the world in an open way trying to trust in a time when human nature is so mangled and corrupt, probably more so than it ever was, where there is no honor, and greed is fashionable. I know the world is wicked; it doesn't shock me anymore. As a matter of fact the thing that stuns and shocks me is human kindness; I see so very little."

In Mitchell's songs, the mixture of direct speech and more abstract imagery that she admired in "Positively Fourth Street" remains a hallmark of her writing. Matching these different lyrical styles with the right sections of the melody, she explained, is a matter of listening closely to the song as it unfolds. "Sometimes the words come first, and then it's easier, because you know exactly what melodic inflection is needed. Given the melody first, you can say, for instance, 'OK, in the A section, I can get away with narrative, descriptive. In the B, I can only speak directly, because of the way the chords are moving. I have to make a direct statement. And in the C section, the chords are so sincere and heartrending that what I say has to be kind of profound, even to myself.' Theatrically speaking, the scene is scored—now you have to put in the dialogue.

"Also, it has to be married to the inflection of English speech," Mitchell said. "Pop music doesn't carry this fine point very far, although a lot of great simple songs do. You know, [*sings*] 'Yesterday.' That's a good melody; that's a good marriage of words and melody, just that simple little piece." To underscore the point, Mitchell sang another example from a work in progress. "OK, you sing: 'Since I lost you' [*sings phrase with melody rising on 'you'*]. But if you go [*sings the same words with melody rising on 'lost'*], the melody puts the emphasis on the word *lost*. And [*sings with long-held note on 'I'*] puts the emphasis on the word *I*. You don't want the emphasis on the word *I*. So a lot of times, even though I may have written the text symmetrically verse to verse to verse, in terms of syncopation I'll sing a slightly different melody to make the emphasis fall on the correct word in the sentence, as you would in spoken English."

Throughout the interview, Mitchell described her vocal craft by using the language of theater, just as she explained her sense of harmony in terms of painting. Metaphorically, these two art forms make a lot of sense together: the chord movement is the painting of the stage scenery—the context and structure of the music—and in the vocal parts, the artist steps onto the stage to act out the part she has scripted for herself. Mitchell's goal as a singer, like that of a good actor, is to embody the words and rise above what she called the "emotional fakery" of pop music.

"Pop music in particular, but music in general, is full of falseness, just loaded with it," Mitchell said. "Blessedly, most people don't hear it, otherwise none of the stuff would be popular. It's contrived, false sexualness in the voice, false sorrow in the voice." This quality is as true

of instrumental music as it is of vocal music, Mitchell said, and she recalled a conversation with Charles Mingus shortly before his death in 1979, when they were collaborating on what became her *Mingus* album. "Mingus at the end, when I went to work with him, couldn't listen to anything except a couple of Charlie Parker records. He kept saying [*imitates deep, raspy voice*], 'That ain't shit. He's falsifying his emotions. Pretentious motherfucker.' Charlie could hear it; I could hear it. He couldn't stand to listen to most of his records because he could perceive in the note the egocenteredness of a player. It's not pleasant to have that perception."

Mitchell cited another example of the importance of the singer's attitude and sincerity, from the sessions for the follow-up to *Turbulent Indigo*. "I'm doing these vocals," she said, "for this song called 'No Apologies.' It's a heavy song. I've had to take four passes at it because it's so heavy that if I color it with any attitude it makes me want to get up and shut it off. I [have to] sing it absolutely deadpan, because it's got such strong language in it."

Beyond the lead vocal, Mitchell often builds elaborate backup vocal parts—usually her own voice multitracked many times over—that amplify or comment on the lyrics in highly unusual ways. Her explanation of where this idea came from, like so many of her explanations, takes us back many layers and many years. "When I was a child, at the age of nine I had polio, and I was paralyzed," she said. "There was no certainty that I would walk again. While I was in the polio ward, it was near Christmas, and I got a coloring book from somebody but no colors. We had these cankers in our mouths, and they would come and paint them with gentian violet and leave these purple swabs behind. So I colored everything light purple and dark purple in the books. My mother put a Christmas tree in the room, and they let me keep it on past curfew one night, and I said to the tree, 'I am not a cripple.' And I said to someone, God or Jesus, I don't remember, 'Give me back my legs and I'll make it up to you.'

"So when my ability to stand and walk primitively returned, they let me leave the hospital, and as soon as I could walk, which was about a year later, I joined the church choir. I took on the descant part, which I called 'the pretty melody.' Most people couldn't sing it because it jumped around too much. Most people—kids, anyway, in a children's choir—couldn't hold onto a note much beyond a third spread; these had five- and seven- and eight-note spreads. [The descant parts] wove all the tighter harmonies of the choral piece together. So from there I got a very unusual melodic sense."

Mitchell considers some of her songs with complex vocal arrangements to be, first and foremost, choral pieces. One example is "The Reoccurring Dream" (from *Chalk Mark in a Rain Storm*), in which background voices chant the seductive messages of advertising: "Latest styles and colors!" "I want a new truck—more power!" "More fulfilling—and less frustrating!" In "The Sire of Sorrow (Job's Sad Song)," the masterful closing work of *Turbulent Indigo*, the background voices are, according to Mitchell, "actually characters—they're the antagonists. They have the insulting lines that these so-called friends of Job's say to him. They augment the drama."

Another example of Mitchell's elaborate dramatic conceptions of her vocal parts is "Slouching towards Bethlehem" (*Night Ride Home*), in which she adapted William Butler Yeats' famous poem "The Second Coming" and added some new words of her own. Of the background vocals, she said, "Conceptually speaking, I wanted it to sound like a global women's lament, so I sang some of the backgrounds with the flatted African palate and some of them with an Arabic kind of [*sings warbling sound*]. I set myself up theatrical assignments like that. Whether or not I achieved that is debatable. To me I did, but then I know what the concept was and what the goal was; other people listening to it maybe think [the voices] are just not very attractive."

Mitchell took a similar type of risk in the dissonant vocal harmonies in "Ethiopia" (*Dog Eat Dog*), a portrait of environmental devastation. "I had a girlfriend say, 'I just hate those harmonies,' and she squeezed her face all up," Mitchell recalled. "I said, 'Why?' and she said, 'You can't use parallel seconds.' I said, 'Well, they said, "You can't use parallel fifths" to Beethoven. You've got these women with dried-up milk glands and cadaverous babies with flies all over them, migrating to God knows what end across a burning desert. You think they're going to sing in a nice major triad?'"

On occasion, Mitchell extends the dramatic scope of a song by using guest singers. She said, "I'll need another voice to deliver a line, because [the songs] are like little plays. Like in 'Dancin' Clown' [*Chalk Mark*], Billy Idol plays the bully. He's got the perfect bully's voice. He's threatening this guy named Jesse [*imitates his voice*]: 'You're a push-button window! I can run you up and down. Anytime I want I can make you my dancing clown!' So you need an aggressive, bullyish voice to deliver that line." On that same album, Willie Nelson makes a much more low-key sort of cameo on "Cool Water," the classic song by the Sons of the Pioneers' Bob Nolan. Nelson's voice, Mitchell said, is "perfect for that song. That was a swing country era. Willie is of that era, and he's got that same kind of beautiful voice. He also sounds like an old desert rat, which is theatrically appropriate for that song."

When you take these sophisticated ideas related to the vocal and lyrical aspects of a song, and lay them on top of expansive harmonies based on ever-changing guitar tunings, the possibilities of songwriting widen to a spectacularly broad horizon. Where most songwriters aim to graft distinctive words or a unique twist of melody onto a tried-and-true song structure or arrangement, Mitchell takes far more risks and far more responsibility. To extend her theatrical metaphor, she is set designer, stage manager, star actor, and supporting cast all in one.

ORCHESTRAL MANEUVERS

Joni Mitchell's first five albums are essentially solo works, driven by her guitar, dulcimer, piano, and voice. But the pared-down production wasn't a reflection of a back-to-basics philosophy, as one might have guessed. "There were no drummers or bass players who could play my music," she said. "I tried the same sections that Carole King and James Taylor were using. I couldn't get on the airwaves because there was no bass and drums on [my records], so I had incentive, but everything they added was arbitrary. They were imposing style on something without seeing what the something was that they were playing to. I thought, 'They're putting big, dark polka dots along the bottom of the music, and fence posts.' I'd end up trying to tell them how to play, and they'd say, 'Isn't it cute, she's telling me how to play my ax, and I've played with James Brown. . . .' So it was difficult as a female to guide males into playing [what I wanted], and to make observations in regard to the music that they had not made. Finally a drummer said, 'Joni, you're going to have to play with jazz musicians.' So I started scouting the clubs, and I found the L.A. Express, but that was for my sixth album [*Court and Spark*]. It took me that long.

"You have to understand, not only was it difficult to be a woman in the business at that time, but the camps of music were very isolated from one another. Jazzers and rockers and folkies did not mix, and I had moved through all of these camps. I was moving into the jazz camp. As far as the rockers were concerned, that was betrayal, and definitely to the folkies. But [jazz musicians] could write out lead sheets; they also could analyze my chords. They were kind of snobbish at first when they heard the music, but when they wrote out what the chord was, they were surprised, because it would be like A sus diminished—these were not normal chords. In standard tuning these chords are very difficult. They would come around with kind of a different respect, or a curiosity at least."

As Mitchell began to work with full-band arrangements, she still maintained strict control over the parts. For *Court and Spark,* she said, "I sang all the countermelody to a scribe, who wrote it out. So anything that's added is my composition. In a few exceptions I'll cut a player loose, but then I'll edit him, move him around, so even though he's given me free lines I'm still collaging them into place. That's why my recording process takes a while. While I hear a certain amount of it in my head, a certain amount of the details are trial and error, because I don't know any of the instruments in what I would call an intellectual way. Not that I'm not storing data—I certainly am, opinions—but I don't know what key I'm in. I can find out by going to the piano, but I generally don't care what key I'm in or if I'm staying in that key. For instance, 'Amelia,' because of the tuning, goes restlessly between two keys. If you wrote it out, you'd have to keep setting up the treble clef and changing the key signature in the middle of every verse and then settling it back in. That is considered by some eccentric—certainly in pop music it is. But it gives the piece a haunting and fresh chordal and melodic movement.

"I've tried to remain true to my own compositional instincts by eliminating the producer, who laminates you to the popular sounds of your time. I've been in conflict with the popular sounds of my time, for the most part. All through the '70s I never liked the sound of the bass or the drums, just on a sonic level, but I couldn't get any [drummers] to take the pillow out of their kick and I couldn't get [bassists] to put fresh strings on and give me a resonant sound, because they were scared to be unhip. Hip is a herd mentality, and it's very conservative, especially among boys."

Mitchell's dissatisfaction with the standard bass sounds of the '70s eventually led to one of the most extraordinary collaborations of her career. "Finally, someone said, 'There's this kid in Florida named Jaco Pastorius. He's really weird; you'd probably like him.' So I sent for Jaco, and he had the sound I was looking for—big and fat and resonant."

The interplay of Mitchell's guitar and Pastorius' bass, first heard on *Hejira*, is a marvel. Pastorius both expands on her chords and harmonics and weaves melodies around her vocal line (including several Stravinsky quotes). His rhythmic/melodic approach, which revolutionized the world of the electric bass, was so thick and up-front that it demanded new approaches on Mitchell's side. "Although I wanted a wide bass sound, his was even wider, and he insisted that he be mixed up so that I was like his background singer," she said. "So to get enough meat to hold his sound, I doubled the guitar loosely—I just played it twice."

Years later, in the recording of *Chalk Mark in a Rain Storm* (1988), Mitchell carried this concept to its extreme, taking advantage of developments in studio technology that allowed the recording of 48 tracks—two 24-track tapes linked together. "I decided to use up one of the reels of the tape doubling the part 24 times. 'My Secret Place' is 24 guitars playing the same part," she said. Her reason for this experiment says as much about her adventurousness as a musician as it does about her obsession with defying categorizations. "On that whole album, all of the guitars are played 24 or 16 times, not in order to get a [Phil] Spector sound but to get people to hear my guitar playing. I thought, 'Well, maybe it's just too thin and silvery sounding. If I beef it up and make a whole section of the guitars, maybe they'll notice how these chords are moving and stop calling it folk music.'"

Over the course of our conversation, Mitchell hammered home this point about labeling again and again. "When they call you a folksinger, they look and they don't listen," she explained. "They see a girl with a guitar, they say folksinger, and they don't listen. It's inhibiting their perception to put that label on it, or to call it jazz—it isn't jazz. Anytime you put a pigeonhole on it, you just see the pigeonhole. It's like almost as soon as you can name, 'Oh, that's a tree,' you almost don't see it anymore. You just see T R E E."

During the recording of *Blue*, she added, "I had kind of a ten-hour period where my vocabulary dumped from stress, and I didn't have a word in my head. It was terrifying, but I'll tell you, when you don't have a word in your head you go back to infancy, and you see water is so watery. When you try to remember the name for water and the name for sand and the name for clouds, by God you really see these boiling things. Once the label has been taken off them, you see their is-ness. So people are not seeing the is-ness of my guitar playing by calling me a folksinger."

A NEAR ENDING AND A NEW BEGINNING

Alternate guitar tunings not only helped to shape Mitchell's voice as a songwriter; they nearly drove her out of the business as well. During the course of the '70s, she recalled, "I began to perform less and less because it seemed like I was spending half my time on stage tuning. I never listened to the applause; I used the time between—the longer they applauded, the more in tune I could get. I just was always frustrated, because if you're singing to a guitar with one note out [of tune] of the six, it'll color the chord and you'll have to go with it, so your vocal pitch is also affected. So the whole thing was frustrating me on all levels—not to mention just the general corruption of the business." Another major factor in her frustration was clearly the souring of her critical reputation and relations with the press—she still recalls slights from *Rolling Stone* and other publications dating back to the '60s and '70s as if they were in this morning's newspaper.

For all these reasons, Mitchell stopped touring in 1983 and performed only intermittently, a retreat from direct contact with her audience that surely heightened her sensitivity to critics' barbs and the swings of pop music fashion. Meanwhile, in the studio, she continued to experiment through the '80s, making heavy use of technology, especially in the synthesizer-based *Dog Eat Dog*. On *Night Ride Home* (1991), her acoustic guitar rose again in the mix, paving the way for its full return in *Turbulent Indigo*, a masterpiece of instrumental understatement that ranks as some of the most haunting work of her career.

Still, none of these developments alleviated Mitchell's difficulties with performing and the business, and her appearance at the 1995 New Orleans Jazz Festival was intended to be her swan song. Enter her old friend Fred Walecki, who saw a possible technological solution to her persistent problems with tunings.

Walecki, of Westwood Music in Los Angeles, designed a lightweight Stratocaster-style guitar to work with the Roland VG-8—the Virtual Guitar—a very sophisticated processor capable of electronically creating her tunings. While the strings physically stay in standard tuning, the VG-8 tweaks the pickup signals so that they come out of the speakers in an altered tuning. This means that Mitchell could use one guitar on stage, with an off-stage tech punching in the preprogrammed tuning for each song. A week before the appearance in New Orleans, Mitchell tried out the new guitar and immediately determined to use it at that gig—much to the horror of Joel Bernstein, who would be there on the side of the stage trying to ensure that this untested prototype instrument using brave-new-world technology would function properly in front of a teeming festival audience.

And somehow, miraculously, it did function properly. Mitchell was aglow about the experience, and she quickly decided that maybe more performing could be in her future after all.

"This new guitar that I'm working with eliminated a certain amount of problems that I had with the acoustic guitar," Mitchell explained. "*Problems* isn't even the right word; *maddening frustrations* is more accurate. The guitar is intended to be played in standard tuning; the neck is calibrated and everything. Twiddling it around isn't good for the instrument, generally speaking. It's not good for the neck; it unsettles the intonation. I have very good pitch, so if I'm never quite in tune, that's frustrating." Over the years, Mitchell has learned to slightly bend the strings to compensate for the intonation error, but that effort is still often defeated by the extreme slackness of her tunings. "In some of those tunings I've got an A on the bottom or a B♭, and it's banging against the string next to it and kicking the thing out of tune as I play, no matter how carefully I tweak it." The VG-8 sidesteps all these problems: as long as the strings are accurately in standard tuning, she can play all over the neck in the virtual alternate tunings and sound in tune.

Mitchell plays her VG-8 guitar, which electronically creates her alternate tunings.

In every gig since the New Orleans Jazz Festival, Mitchell has used the VG-8, using its effects to build a guitar sound reminiscent of her *Hejira*

era. But the VG-8 is having a much larger impact on her music than just providing a workable stage setup. In composing and recording the songs for her next album [*Taming the Tiger*], she's thrown herself into a heady exploration of the VG-8's sampled sounds. "Sonically, it's very new," she said of the tracks recorded so far. "I don't know what you'd call it. It's my impression, in a way, of '40s music. Because I don't like a lot of contemporary music, I kind of cleared my ear and didn't listen to anything for a while, and what emerged were these vague memories of '40s and early '50s sounds. Swinging brass—not Benny Goodman and not Glenn Miller but my own brand, pulled through Miles [Davis] and different harmonic stuff that I absorbed in the '50s. Because this guitar has heavy-metal sounds in it and pretty good brass sounds, I'm mixing heavy-metal sounds with a brass section, so it's a really strange hybrid kind of music. I'm a bit scared of it sometimes, you know. I don't know what it is."

While removing certain variables from Mitchell's guitar, the VG-8 does, in fact, introduce some new ones. The sounds, she said, "rock around. They settle and they throw out these digital freak-outs—it's like Jimi Hendrix feedback. Some of it's beautiful and some of it isn't. I don't know live what's going to happen. It's not reliable, because I tend to rake the strings; I don't have the light touch of an electric player. I'm adapting my touch to this new instrument; I'm having to gentle it down a lot, 'cause I don't have to make it bark by physically yanking it, like I did before. The electricity will take care of it. However, when you do yank it like that, you get these colorful and sometimes splendid accidents, because you confuse the brain."

The richest irony of Mitchell's VG-8 experience thus far is that this guitar rig, which was intended to make her alternate tunings more practical and usable, has in fact driven her to write her first song in 30 years in standard tuning! A technical barrier is responsible: the VG-8's samples were created to be used with a guitar in standard tuning,

DISCOGRAPHY

Both Sides Now, Reprise 47640 (2000)

Taming the Tiger, Reprise 46451 (1998).

Hits, Reprise 46326 (1996).

Misses, Reprise 46358 (1996).

Big Yellow Taxi (The Remixes), Reprise 43600 (1996).

Turbulent Indigo, Reprise 45786 (1994).

Night Ride Home, Geffen 24302 (1991).

Chalk Mark in a Rain Storm, Geffen 24172 (1988).

Dog Eat Dog, Geffen 24074 (1985).

Wild Things Run Fast, Geffen 2019 (1982).

Shadows and Light, Asylum BC5-704 (1980).

Mingus, Asylum 505 (1979).

Don Juan's Reckless Daughter, Asylum 701 (1977).

Hejira, Asylum 1087 (1976).

The Hissing of Summer Lawns, Asylum 1051 (1975).

Miles of Aisles, Asylum 202 (1974).

Court and Spark, Asylum 1001 (1974).

For the Roses, Asylum 5057 (1972).

Blue, Reprise 2038 (1971).

Ladies of the Canyon, Reprise 6376 (1970).

Clouds, Reprise 6351 (1969).

Joni Mitchell, Reprise 6293 (1968).

WHAT THEY PLAY (1996)

Joni Mitchell has never quite gotten over the first guitar she loved and lost: a '56 Martin D-28 she got circa 1966 from a Marine captain stationed at Fort Bragg, North Carolina. The guitar had accompanied him to Vietnam and was in his tent when it was hit with shrapnel. "There were two instruments and all this captain's stuff in there," Mitchell says. "When they cleared the wreckage, all that survived was this guitar. I don't know whether the explosion did something to the modules in the wood, but that guitar was a trooper, man." Mitchell played that D-28 on all her early albums. Before she recorded *Court and Spark,* it was damaged on an airline, and soon after it was stolen off a luggage carousel in Maui. Wistfully, she adds, "I've never found an acoustic that could compare with it."

As Mitchell explored jazzier sounds in the late '70s, she turned to electric guitars. From 1979 until the mid-'80s, she performed with five George Benson model Ibanez guitars, which were set up by Joel Bernstein and Larry Cragg with a range of string gauges to accommodate her tunings. At that time, the Roland Jazz Chorus amplifier—which was invented, Mitchell says, so she could replicate her *Hejira* sound in performance—was an important component of her live sound.

These days, Mitchell's main acoustics are a Martin D-45, a Martin D-28, and two Collings—a D2H and a petite custom model—that she calls "the best acoustic guitars I've found since I lost my dear one." She says, "I need really good intonation, and one of the signs of really good intonation is how flashy the harmonics are with a light touch. You should be able to get them to bloom like jewels. Both those guitars have that capacity. Of the two, the big one [which was the primary guitar for *Turbulent Indigo*] records better, but the little one is so sweet to cradle. It's just the right size for sitting. I write a lot on it and I travel with it, which is kind of scary. I carry it on board with me, because I won't take a chance on it. I won't let it go into the hold and get mushed like my beloved."

Since 1995, Mitchell has almost exclusively played a MIDI electric guitar made by Fred Walecki of Westwood Music in Los Angeles, which she uses with the Roland VG-8 processor to electronically create her alternate tunings. The guitar is made with a very lightweight yellow spruce body (because heavy guitars give her problems on stage, a lingering effect of childhood polio) and a neck that's somewhere between that of a Martin and a Stratocaster.

and initially they were not accessible in conjunction with her alternate tunings (Roland has since fixed this problem).

So Mitchell's first VG-8 composition, "Harlem in Havana," is in that vaguely remembered thing called standard tuning. "You'd never know it was in standard tuning because I haven't played in standard tuning for 30 years," she said. "I don't know how to play in standard tuning, so I treated standard tuning like it was a new tuning and used my repertoire of shapes.

"It's a strange piece of music. The guitar sound that I'm using is like a marimba, but it's not like any marimba part you've ever heard because it's fingerpicked. The bass string is almost atonal and sounds almost like a didgeridoo. But off of it I'm building huge horn sections, and the poem that's going to it is about two little girls in my hometown getting into this black revue called *Harlem in Havana*, which was an Afro-Cuban burlesque kind of show that you weren't supposed to stand in front of, let alone go in."

As Mitchell continues to work on the album that she called "probably the biggest break for me since *Court and Spark*," a number of other projects are percolating. A best-of collection is in the works [*Hits* and *Misses*, released in 1996], and the VG-8 seems to be encouraging her tentative steps back onto the stage—in November '95, she played her first full-length gig in years, at the Fez in New York. Further into the future, we can look forward to a new CD anthology and a complete songbook, with all the tunings and basic chord shapes. That book will be an invaluable map for retracing the steps of one of the most amazing songwriting journeys of our time, while Joni Mitchell herself disappears around the next bend.

Jerry Garcia (left)
and David Grisman.

JERRY GARCIA
AND DAVID GRISMAN

In the last few years of his life, Jerry Garcia spent a lot of time hanging

out in the home studio of mandolin master David Grisman—jamming,

renewing an old friendship, and reconnecting with the acoustic

instruments and American roots styles that originally inspired his life in

music. It was the perfect bookend to his three-decade journey with the

Grateful Dead, a warm last chorus of some favorite old songs.

Grisman was always rolling tape during those sessions, and

at the time of this conversation in the fall of 1993, two fine albums had

already come of them: *Jerry Garcia/David Grisman* and *Not for Kids*

Only. Garcia was in a festive mood, clearly enjoying his acoustic

re-education with his old picking pal, and his childlike enthusiasm

made a memorable contrast to the more curmudgeonly (although no

less enthusiastic) Grisman. Garcia's health, too, seemed to be on the upswing, but just shy of two years later the catalog of abuses suffered by his body caught up with him, cutting his life short when his spirit seemed to want to go on forever.

Thanks to Grisman's incredible archive of master tapes, the Garcia/Grisman discography has continued to grow, with the folk-song collection *Shady Grove,* the jazz set *So What,* and *The Pizza Tapes,* which documents a hang-loose jam with flatpicking guitar legend Tony Rice that was bootlegged for years and then finally released in "official" form in 2000. Even Garcia and Grisman's brief early '70s bluegrass project Old and in the Way has been resurrected, with two more CDs of live performances.

It is poignant to realize that some of the projects discussed in this interview never happened, although it's also hard to imagine *any* musician leaving us with as much soulful music as did Jerry Garcia.

IN THE DAWG HOUSE

His touch on the instrument is instantly recognizable, all his own, like the one-of-a-kind sound of his band. For more than 30 years, he has explored American music traditions and blended them into new forms, creating along the way his own niche within the music industry rather than conforming to existing molds. His passion and energy for music seem inexhaustible; he's got enough projects on the drawing board to last a few more lifetimes.

All of these things could be said about both Jerry Garcia and David Grisman. Since they first met as bluegrass seekers in the late '60s, they have traveled in very different directions—Garcia on the Grateful Dead electric rock 'n' roll odyssey, Grisman creating the acoustic string-band style known as Dawg—yet their musical paths have continued to cross ever since. And now, more than two decades after Grisman laid down mandolin tracks on the Grateful Dead's *American Beauty,* and Garcia and Grisman joined with John Kahn, Peter Rowan, and Richard Greene (sometimes replaced by Vassar Clements) to form the short-lived, ever-popular bluegrass band Old and in the Way, Garcia and Grisman are teaming up again to celebrate their acoustic roots and to map out some new acoustic routes for the future.

It's no surprise to find David Grisman in this setting. He has flown the acoustic flag for all of his prolific and extremely influential career, and his growing record label, Acoustic Disc, speaks to his allegiances. As a player, Grisman has set the standard for a new generation of mando-maniacs, and his bands have acted as a training ground for some of the most creative instrumentalists in the acoustic music world—Tony Rice, Mark O'Connor, Mike Marshall, and Darol Anger, to name a few. Garcia's presence behind an acoustic guitar is less common; his fame, as well as the vast majority of his concerts and recordings, stems from his mesmerizing electric guitar work. But Garcia's relationship with acoustic music is deep and complex. From old-time music to bluegrass to early jazz, Garcia shares many acoustic inspirations with Grisman; a short, off-the-top-of-their-heads list includes Django Reinhardt, Stéphane Grappelli, Bill Monroe, Flatt and Scruggs, Riley Puckett, Joe Venuti, Eddie Lang, Roy Smeck, Oscar Alemán, Nick Lucas. . . . And one of the most distinctive aspects of the Grateful Dead, which was born from a jug band, is that its connections to traditional folk and country remain clear and present even in its most outlandish electric jams. The connection is strong enough that a song like "Friend of the Devil," which began life in 1970 as an upbeat bluegrassy tune, could dramatically evolve into a slowed-down electric meditation over the course of many years of Dead shows; and that new identity could translate effortlessly and beautifully back to an acoustic arrangement on the 1991 *Garcia/Grisman* album.

As I sit with Garcia and Grisman in Grisman's home studio in Mill Valley, California, on a sunny September afternoon, it's a wonder to behold the enthusiasm and love these two share for their recent collaborations—and for music of all kinds. Following the *Garcia/Grisman* album, which spanned blues ("The Thrill Is Gone"), country ("Dawg's Waltz"), and Irving Berlin ("Russian Lullaby"), the duo just released a very laid-back, old-timey children's album, *Not for Kids Only,* which travels from "Freight Train" to "Shenandoah" to "Teddy Bear's Picnic." And as you'll see, these projects mark just the beginning of a whole new process of discovery.

Back in the late '60s, when you two first met, you were both on the bluegrass quest, to use David's words from the liner notes to Old and in the Way; *you were searching for that "high lonesome sound" of Bill Monroe and Flatt and Scruggs. Both of you have covered a lot of musical ground since then. Are you still on that quest?*

GARCIA It's funny you should mention that, because we were thinking of starting to work on a bluegrass album sometime in the future.

GRISMAN Yeah, I want to put Jerry back in the bluegrass business.

GARCIA I love having an excuse to play bluegrass music. I have to work my chops up, because I can't stand to play the banjo for no reason. There has to be something coming up, a chance to play the music. It would be fun to do.

Would you play all banjo, or would you do some guitar as well?

GARCIA I'd probably do the guitar. I never was a very good bluegrass guitar player—I was a banjo player when I played—but I think I could take a whack at some guitar stuff, maybe now that David's got my acoustic chops up to where they are almost mediocre [*laughs*].

GRISMAN On the tone level, he's up there with anybody.

In what ways would a project like this be different than when you played bluegrass together before?

GARCIA We would play with interesting people—that would be the fun part of it.

GRISMAN I'd like to get Jerry and Ralph Stanley together. I think they'd sing some mighty powerful duets.
    I get to play with some of the masters of the idiom, and it kind of spoils you for the rest of it. There's something about the original guys and their original disciples. . . . Bluegrass is a kind of music, for me, that came out of a certain time and place—between 1948 and 1958 in the Southeast, basically. It has that vibe to it. There are a lot of great guys younger than us who have come along and are the standard bearers of bluegrass now, and they've taken it technically to some new plateaus, but—

GARCIA —the spirit of the original stuff is the real thing; that's what really works on an emotional level. It has something like soul or heart or spirit or some invisible element, some X quantity. Those original guys had it well enough so that it turns up on a lot of recordings. The recordings were mostly one-shots, recorded at odd times in funky studios, and even through [those circumstances], the performances have that quality.

GRISMAN A certain kind of innocence, or impoverishment, or whatever it was.

GARCIA Yeah, the thing of playing it for real, playing it as good as they could play. And they believed in it.

GRISMAN Plus it was really untouched. These people were in their own world.
    Something has changed in bluegrass. I guess it's probably like anything: the original flash of something is *it*. Like Robert Johnson. And we were fortunate to be close enough to the birth of this art form, or the golden age of

it, and got to see some of the real people do it and even play with some of those people.

GARCIA Yeah! To get that hit, the real hit, the authentic hit, the where-it-comes-from hit.

GRISMAN I made this record a few years ago, *Home Is Where the Heart Is.* I wanted to do it with all older guys, and we just couldn't get enough of them, so I brought in some of the younger guys. But still, it was a lot of fun, and I've been telling Jerry he could have a similar amount of fun.

From what I understand, Old and in the Way *is one of the best-selling bluegrass albums ever.*

GARCIA I've heard that, and I wonder if that's true. I can't believe that it sold more than the Nitty Gritty Dirt Band.

GRISMAN That's the hype. I'm sure now it's not [the best-seller], but at some point it was.

Still, I think it's true that for a lot of people, Old and in the Way *is the only bluegrass album in their collection.*

GARCIA That's flattering.

What kind of an image of bluegrass do you think those people are getting, as compared to that original sound you were talking about?

GARCIA The music on *Old and in the Way* is pretty good; I mean it ain't bad. I don't know if I can answer that question; it's really hard to remove yourself.

GRISMAN It's funny, 'cause I was talking to a friend of mine, Mike Garris, who's a younger bluegrass musician. He was playing with Del McCoury's band, and he's a progressive kind of guy. He's a lot younger than us—he was probably 15 years old when *Old and in the Way* came out—and he happened to mention to me that he saw *Old and in the Way* as opening up the door for a lot of progressive elements in bluegrass. We weren't looking at it that way at all. We did some original tunes and a couple of different tunes.

GARCIA Tunes from outside the idiom. We did some unusual things—"The Great Pretender," "Wild Horses" . . .

GRISMAN But really, we didn't start stuff like that. The Country Gentlemen were progressive. . . . We were just trying to play the traditional stuff and adapt some songs. We didn't want to do just covers, and Peter [Rowan] was a songwriter. We weren't trying to do anything but have a bluegrass band.

What sources did you go back to in choosing the tunes for your kids' record?

GRISMAN The New Lost City Ramblers songbook.

GARCIA Right! Most of the ones that we liked, it turns out the New Lost City Ramblers did first. And some of them were just from the great common law book of so-called American folk music. Some of them were just weird things from the children's music pantheon.

Jerry, you commented recently that many kids' songs have been sanitized or divorced from their original sources.

GARCIA That's one of my personal complaints, and I've been using it as a rap to go along with this record. There are these shows and videos that are supposedly for kids, and a lot of it is totally gutless. It doesn't have anything going for it. It's made to be as inoffensive as it could possibly be.

GRISMAN It's pabulum, musical pabulum, which is OK for infants—

GARCIA —but kids like weird shit in there. They like scary stuff lurking around, things with teeth, crazy people.

GRISMAN Plus they get plenty of it on the news and everywhere else on TV.

GARCIA They're realistic. They know that the world is full of weird stuff, and kids sort of prefer weird stuff; they rejoice in it. It's no big thing, but it's nice to be able to throw some music back in there that's originally from that world, bring a little of the weirdness back, take a chance a little. It's sort of trusting that the kids can handle something more than terminal niceness.

How was it working on such simple songs and simple arrangements?

GRISMAN We fall into stuff that just comes easy. I think the first day we knocked out about three of these tunes, and we had never played them. It wasn't like we had to work on them. Just about every tune on here we thought of at the session. We'd just think of them, print out the words, and then do them.

Was the arranging process pretty straightforward, then?

GARCIA We'd find a key that seemed like it was singable and good for my range, and then it's a matter of saying, "Oh, we could do some instrumentals in here maybe" or "We could just throw a lick in here." They start just as roughly the chord changes, the melody, and the lyrics, and the rest of it is put together as we go along.

And then David and his magic razor blade: sometimes he can create an arrangement where there wasn't one!

GRISMAN And then we added stuff to it afterward. We recorded everything ourselves, except one song we recorded with piano and then added a string arrangement to it.

Were you recording mostly live with voice and instruments?

GRISMAN With just the two of us, yeah. We did all that live, and then Jerry went away for a long time and I had nothing to do, so I started overdubbing. I figured that maybe a whole album of just the two of us—

GARCIA —might be a little spare.

GRISMAN I think kids like catchy sounds. So we added some percussion and Jew's harp—not a lot of stuff on any one song. A little harmonica.

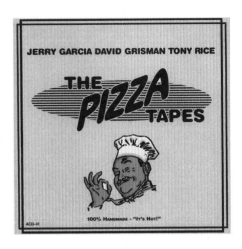

Jerry, you have said that you and David have different working styles: David's more rigorous and disciplined, and you're looser. When you are working out the kind of complex arrangements that were on the Garcia/Grisman *album, how do those styles play off each other?*

GARCIA Well, I'm capable of working on stuff. He can always intimidate me into working on stuff. I don't shrink from it.

GRISMAN Hey, we don't do one take and he says, "That's good enough." When push comes to shove, he's a perfectionist. He's even more finicky about some things than I am. They are personal things: every musician, I think, has to have them.

GARCIA There has to be that guy in you, otherwise your playing is going to be lame.

So when it comes right down to it, you don't see your styles as all that different.

GARCIA No, they're not. We have a pretty harmonious relationship. It's fun—that's the bottom line. The music is fun, and for me it's challenging. I'm enjoying playing acoustic guitar. It's a process of discovery for me. I think I'm getting better at it, and it's gratifying to start to find more levels of it.

When you say "more levels," do you mean things like tone or phrasing?

GARCIA Articulation of every kind. [As for] phrasing, I'm kind of in my own world. There's not that much that I can do about my own choice of notes. But I can work on getting a good sound out of the instrument and being able to individuate the notes more based on all kinds of things—the feel of the instrument, what it's capable of, how well it speaks. Some of these guitars are just remarkable.

GRISMAN He's gotten more into playing vintage guitars.

GARCIA That's a new experience for me. Although I've owned them, I just haven't gotten into playing them a lot. And then having the feedback of

recording them. You listen and think, "Oh, jeez, this guitar has a wonderfully warm midrange."

Compared to when you play electric guitar, do you use open strings more on an acoustic or generally play lower on the neck?

GARCIA I do for accompaniment in this style [of the kids' album]. I like to play a kind of open, old-time guitar style, a real supportive style with structural runs and basic rhythms. You just get a nice, chunky sound.

GRISMAN He knows a lot of traditional ways to play the kinds of music we play. He's not like some rock 'n' roller who only knows three chords, and he knows stuff like Riley Puckett style.

Those traditional styles make different kinds of appearances in the Grateful Dead setting too.

GARCIA Yeah, well, part of it is just my musical personality. I listen to all this music and make a real effort to learn it. I certainly love it.

How much improvisation happens in a more open-ended tune like "Arabia" from Garcia/Grisman?

GRISMAN Well, you can tell the parts that aren't improvised, where we play unison lines. The solos are improvised. I always think that really the only difference between improvisation and composition is a time factor.

GARCIA Yeah, it's fast composition. That's a good point that should be understood.

GRISMAN It's hard to say one is composing and the other is improvising. There's a certain amount of what you "improvise" that's part of your shtick—it's the reason you can recognize Charlie Parker, because he is playing the same stuff every time, in a way.

GARCIA If you've got a recognizable style, that's really your limitations, you know what I mean? Basically, you play what you know how to play. And then within that, sometimes in moments of great clarity, you are able to see stuff that you don't know how to play, but it's close enough to what you do know how to play that you might try for it, and sometimes you might hit it. I tend to do that more often than is probably safe, because I frequently fuck up. Sometimes it works, and if you keep on trying at it, eventually your percentages do improve; but then it just becomes new stuff that you do know how to play.

GRISMAN And there's an area that isn't technically difficult. I always tell people who want to learn how to improvise, it doesn't necessarily have to be complicated. You could improvise in half notes.

But it's the creative process, and what I'm trying to say is that even though we can say it's improvisation, what we played today isn't totally different from what we played yesterday. I don't think anybody just improvises something that they've never heard before, unless they're somebody like [pianist] Cecil Taylor—I wouldn't really imagine that he knows what he's playing half the time, in other words that he could write it down.

GARCIA You'd have to be somebody like [saxophonist] Sonny Rollins, playing all solo without any structure to follow, so you're free of all the structures of familiar combinations of chords. If you subtract all that, and you're playing without any regard to a structure of any kind, then you might have a shot at free improvisation, and even that's hard to do. Derek Bailey tries to do that. He's an English guitar player, and he plays with all kinds of people like Yo-Yo Ma, Steve Lacy, jazz guys, classical guys, Indian guys, people from every different musical idiom. His playing sounds almost completely random. It's not pretty at all; it's just *stuff.* But he says, "I'm right at least 50 percent of the time." He's got a sort of statistical approach to improvisation, which is interesting. If you're suspending rules, there are no mistakes.

GRISMAN But there are idioms that lend themselves to more free playing or loose playing, like jazz. You can get away with more. Whereas in bluegrass, there's improvisation, but it's got to be within a certain harmonic [framework].

GARCIA Bluegrass is kind of like flamenco, in that the structure is really important—knowing the tunes, how they work, and how the band works. In flamenco, the tunes are everything, and everybody knows all the tunes. The improvisation you do is within a very formal structure, but it's still improvisation.

I prefer form. I think of myself as being kind of conservative on that level. But I also like to play something that's tonal but doesn't necessarily have a lot of structure going for it, because then you can play open and you can do rhythmic ideas that go beyond certain phrase lengths. If you're playing in a chord pattern of a 16-bar song, you're typically stuck with four-bar phrases. You may or may not stick to that structure, but you're going to be conscious of those time intervals; but if you have something wide open, like "Arabia," that has open sections or sections that are modal, then you have an opportunity to play around with the rhythm more intensely, to do weirder things with it.

How would you compare each other's soloing styles?

GRISMAN Compare them?

GARCIA I've always thought of David as being the Bela Lugosi of the mandolin [*Grisman laughs*].

GRISMAN I think of Jerry as the Rondo Hatton of the guitar [*more laughter*].

Let me phrase it this way: Do you think you have very different sensibilities in soloing?

GARCIA David's playing always sounds very fiery to me and Gypsy-esque somehow. That's a real generalization. David can sound kind of Russian to me. But he can sound like anything. When we do "Stealin'" and he does that banjo thing, he sounds like the Memphis Jug Band.

David plays into the music, whatever the music calls for. That's why you could call him into a session for any kind of music, any structure, any band, any instrumentation, and he will play something that's appropriate to the music.

GRISMAN Jerry is one of those guys [from whom] you don't really know what to expect. Sometimes he'll play something real understated and simple, and he favors sometimes the low register of the guitar.

Those low-register melodies are especially unusual on electric guitar.

GRISMAN He's very melodic, but he puts in a lot of accidentals. He's got his own personality; tone is a lot of it. One credit to Jerry is that he's got his own sound with the electric guitar, and it's not the same sound on acoustic guitar—you couldn't put it on an oscilloscope and see that it's the same sound—but it's the same vibe. Which is, I think, pretty amazing.

I've noticed in concerts with your respective bands that you both play a role of provoking things—throwing a curve ball at one of the other players and having them respond.

GARCIA Trying to lose the other members of the band [*laughs*].

How much of that happens when you play together?

GRISMAN We don't play that much together where we want to screw each other up that much—

GARCIA —but just a little bit. It depends on the situation. In reality, we haven't had a chance to play that much together live, to where we've developed even a consistent approach. It's pretty different every time we play. That just means that there are lots of possible ways that we could go. Sometimes I just can't help myself, I just have to follow him somewhere. I have a hard time restraining myself under the best of circumstances.

Sometimes it's like a chess match where you [Grisman] are a couple of moves ahead, and we're both playing a couple of moves ahead! So stuff will come out at extremely weird places. That's part of the fun of it, the element of surprise.

GRISMAN And we'll think of songs. I guess we listened to a lot of the same stuff in our history, and we pull these things out—things that hardly anyone else would know about. Records of sea chanteys from 1961 or something that we both were into.

I'd like to backtrack to 1970, when the Grateful Dead released American Beauty *and* Workingman's Dead, *which are, to my mind, two of the best albums in the Dead catalog. What inspired these acoustically oriented albums amidst all the electric rock that you were experimenting with at the time?*

GARCIA It was very simple. We had gone to such excess with our weirder albums, and we had spent so much money, we were in the hole so deeply, that I said, "We've got to figure out a way to make simpler records, you guys." And I said, "Let's make them straight-ahead, real simple, acoustic guitar, real easy songs, we'll rehearse them a lot, we won't fuck around in the studio." We had spent like eight months in the studio on some of those [earlier] albums, and this was in '66 and '67, when people weren't doing stuff like that.

The thing of *American Beauty* was that David happened to be in town, and there were a couple of tunes that cried out for what David could add to them.

David, what are your recollections of that time?

GRISMAN I was visiting up here in about 1970, and somebody invited me to this baseball game in Fairfax between the Grateful Dead and the Jefferson Airplane.

Who won?

GRISMAN [*Laughs*] I don't remember. So I went there and ran into Jerry, and he said, "I've got a couple of tunes I'd love to have you record."

I was just here on a visit, and actually it's probably the reason I moved out here: I figured, "Wow, I already got a gig." But it was an overdub session, so it was just a couple of hours.

A rare photo of the legendary band Old and in the Way. From left to right: John Kahn, Richard Greene, David Grisman, Peter Rowan, and Jerry Garcia.

And you played at some Dead shows, too, at the time?

GARCIA Yeah, back at the Fillmore East.

GRISMAN I sat in with them once or twice.

GARCIA We even did a kind of re-creation of that album. We played the acoustic instruments, and I even used different guitars on different songs—something I never do on stage.

Also on the subject of Grateful Dead music—

GARCIA Ahh, let's not talk about Grateful Dead music.

OK, just one more question. So much of the Dead's music has been electric, but it always retains some kind of connection to old-time country and folk sounds. For one thing, the songs translate really naturally back to acoustic arrangements.

GARCIA Well, when the Grateful Dead started, three of us in the band were in a jug band together—me and Bob [Weir] and Pig Pen all had some kind of basic grounding in acoustic music of one sort or another. Pig Pen was a Lightning Hopkins nut, and Bob was fingerpicking guitar—he liked Reverend Gary Davis a lot—and I was coming from the bluegrass/country stuff, and blues also. So we crossed over there, and we also all had some knowledge of the great Chess records, the Chicago blues of the '50s. As soon as we heard the Rolling Stones doing all these tunes—Muddy Waters tunes, Chuck Berry tunes—we thought, "We know those tunes. We could do that. It'd be easy to start a rock 'n' roll band. We already know this music, so it's not like we have to learn something. All we need to do is get a drummer and a bass player and we're off to the races." And that's pretty much what we did.

GRISMAN Plus, they did a lot of folk material, like "Cold Rain and Snow." They adapted a bunch of tunes.

I'd like to ask a couple of questions about recording. Jerry, you've described frustrations in the past—at least in the Grateful Dead context—about trying to translate the live sound into the studio. How does this literally down-home recording environment work for you?

GARCIA This is really fun. We're playing the music, and we're not doing a whole lot of overdubbing—in fact almost none. David likes it that way, and I like it that way too.

GRISMAN I just don't like the attitude of some musicians, "Well, this is a scratch vocal." In other words, this is somehow less than what we're gonna do when it really comes time. I think, "Hey, if you're a musician, you put it down now." If there's some reason that it didn't work, then you go back and fix it. And there's some intangible thing about a performance, even if it's got mistakes. It's an entity.

GARCIA The most successful Grateful Dead record was the one that we approached kind of this way, by really performing the tunes—*In the Dark*. We actually performed the tunes, vocals and everything, and we fixed them up if there was something wrong with them, but the performances were fundamentally live—not live with an audience, but live in the sense that we all played at the same time.

GRISMAN It's just a different ethic with musicians [today]. Before all the multitracking came in, they weren't even aware that there was any way to fix it. You just went and played it. The first records I made were in mono, and whatever was done was done at the time, and it just made you strive higher, I think.

GARCIA The fix-it mentality is one of the reasons why so many records are so mediocre and boring. Or even worse, there's the idea that even if there's no song, we can construct one if we just start with a groove. It's that mechanistic. It's not music at all, it's like building a model airplane.

GRISMAN I was doing a session here on another project, and I won't say who it was, but one of the musicians says, "Well, I'd like to do my part later." I was the producer, and what it really meant was that I was going to have to come back later and spend more time. And I said, "Look, what if everyone here said that? There would be no record."

GARCIA Yeah, I have that beef. Sometimes in the Grateful Dead we have a tug-of-war along those lines about what's the best way to do it. And the attitude that you build it a bit at a time is prevalent in the Grateful Dead because of the fix-it mentality. But on this record, the Grateful Dead record coming up, I'm going to want to do it by performing them. Now that we do this thing with the earphones, it's actually more feasible.

How do you use the earphones?

GARCIA We use earphones instead of monitors on stage now. We don't have any speakers on stage anymore.

Does the fact that you have your own label, David, free you to record the way you want? In other words, are the record companies putting the pressure on people to record in the piecemeal way you're describing?

GARCIA I don't think record companies put any pressure on.

GRISMAN Well, I think they do at a certain stage.

GARCIA They want product.

GRISMAN But they often have things to say about the product.

GARCIA They don't with us very much.

GRISMAN Yeah, but you're in a different position. They don't do it to me very much either, but probably for different reasons, probably because they don't understand—

GARCIA No, it's basically the same reason. They don't understand us either [*laughs*]. I guess they push around who they can.

GRISMAN Well, if they don't push you around artistically, they certainly say, "We want a record now" or, "We don't want a record now." With my own record company, there's nobody to ask if I can do something, unless I want to do something really expensive. I still wouldn't have to ask anybody; I'd just have to make sure I could afford it.

I've had not a lot but some problems with various record labels. And mostly the problem is that the things I do are just not in the mainstream. Nobody's really going to go to bat for it because they don't really understand it. It's music that slips through the cracks, so to speak. There's not a category for it. One guy calls it country, and the next guy calls it jazz, but in the meantime I'm not in either one. It's a problem in marketing. Record companies

SELECTED DISCOGRAPHY

JERRY GARCIA AND DAVID GRISMAN
The Pizza Tapes (with Tony Rice),
  Acoustic Disc 41 (2000).
So What, Acoustic Disc 33 (1998).
Shady Grove, Acoustic Disc 21 (1996).
Not for Kids Only, Acoustic Disc 9 (1994).
Jerry Garcia/David Grisman,
  Acoustic Disc 2 (1992).

OLD AND IN THE WAY
Breakdown, Acoustic Disc 28 (1997).
That High Lonesome Sound,
  Acoustic Disc 19 (1996).
Old and in the Way, Rykodisc
  10009 (originally released 1975).

GRATEFUL DEAD (ACOUSTIC)
Reckoning, Arista 8523 (1981).
History of the Grateful Dead ("Bear's
  Choice"), Warner Bros. 2721 (1974).
Workingman's Dead, Warner Bros.
  1869 (1970).
American Beauty, Warner Bros. 1893
  (1970).

JERRY GARCIA ACOUSTIC BAND
Almost Acoustic, Grateful Dead
  4005 (1988).

don't think along individual music lines; they want to be able to lump and package something together. They don't want something that could be in three markets; they want it in one market.

GARCIA They want it demographically identifiable.

GRISMAN When I was with MCA, they wanted me to make a jazz record with jazz names. But I had a band, you know, and I was playing my music; finally I was ready to make a record, and they said, "Well, we want to hear the tunes." At that point nobody had asked me to hear the tunes for many years, so I said, "Hey, the hell with this. You can listen to all my other records, and either you want to hear the next one or you don't."

Actually, I have recorded for lots of labels, and the smaller ones, by and large, have hassled me more than the larger ones. With the larger ones, really it's all about business; you can either sell enough records for them to be happy or not. But most of the people who start the smaller labels are would-be musicians or people who want to get involved with certain kinds of music.

I'll tell you, this *Here Today* record—it's a bluegrass album that Herb Pedersen and Jimmy Buchanan and Vince Gill made about 12 years ago—Rounder Records just put it out on CD, and we did that song "Making Plans"—remember that Osborne Brothers song? There's a lick that Sonny Osborne played on a banjo at the end; it's a turnaround where he plays some kind of augmented lick, a modern chord [*sings notes*]. Remember that?

GARCIA Sure do.

GRISMAN Well, we did the same thing on our record. They just put out a CD, and they cut out that chord and pasted in another chord.

GARCIA You're kidding. Unbelievable! What gall!

GRISMAN Isn't that incredible?

GARCIA The way Arista works, Clive Davis, if you ask him, he will invent an opinion, but apart from that he doesn't have one and he wouldn't volunteer one.

We don't sell that many records, but they like us on the label because we're a prestige act. We're high visibility.

David, since you have the studio here, do you find that you record a lot more?

WHAT THEY PLAY (GRISMAN, 1993)

David Grisman has a large and varied collection of mandolin-family instruments. On stage and on record, Grisman usually plays either his 1922 Lloyd Loar Gibson F-5 or his Gilchrist Model 5, which he says is "like a baby F-5." On *Not for Kids Only,* Grisman played a lot of round-hole mandolins that he wouldn't normally use in the studio. "To me they sound a little earthier or more homespun," he says. "You can appreciate them more with just guitar and mandolin, because they're kind of deeper in a way, a wider kind of sound that gets soaked up with other instruments."

On all his instruments, Grisman uses D'Addario strings and heavy, rounded flatpicks made by Saga (formerly sold as David Grisman picks, now as Golden Gate picks). "I've lowered my action a lot since when I was playing bluegrass," Grisman says, "because I used to have to play with banjo players. Volume was a virtue, and still is to a certain extent, but I like to play quiet, because it's a better sound. You're really in control of it."

That philosophy extends to the amplification of Grisman's bands, in which he tries to maintain the natural acoustic balance rather than compensate for volume imbalances with the PA. "When I started my band, we used to play gigs with no PAs. Tony Rice was always pissed off, because the guitar, let's face it, is a bad design," Grisman says with a laugh. "It doesn't cut like a mandolin or a fiddle. Basically, I think [good sound] comes from natural dynamics. If somebody's quiet, you back off and make sure that you can hear him."

In the studio and on stage, Grisman plays through Neumann KM-84 mics, and he's always been an evangelist for using mics over pickups. "It's a tonal thing for me," he says. "I love that acoustic sound, and I think it needs some protagonists out there. I just don't think I have a sound on an electric—my sound is acoustic. You take that away and I'm kind of lost." At Quintet gigs, Grisman has tried putting two mics each on the guitar and the bass, and he says that technique improved their sound.

In Grisman's home studio—which is basically transplanted from the Berkeley, California, studio where he recorded many of his early Quintet albums—he uses a 3M eight-track analog recorder. With close miking and baffles, he achieves a good enough separation that tracks recorded together live can be replaced if necessary. Grisman has a DAT machine as well but prefers the analog sound, so he mainly uses the DAT for making rough mixes and copies. The eight-track is mixed down to a Fostex half-inch reel-to-reel machine, from which the digital master is made for reproduction.

GRISMAN Yeah, I record a lot of stuff here that's not for any record. Like I did a project with Tony Rice that's going to be coming out, and I invited Jerry over to meet Tony. Jerry came over, and we recorded probably 12 or 13 tunes, just the three of us [*that session was eventually bootlegged—and then released—as* The Pizza Tapes].

I've been working on a project that's probably going to be called *Dawg Duos*, just recording duets with different musicians who pass through. I've been accumulating them now for two or three years. Vassar [Clements] has been here, John Hartford, Edgar Meyer. . . .

Do you have someone here to engineer those sessions?

GRISMAN I have an engineer, Dave Dennison, Decibel Dave. He's real good, he's my protégé.

GARCIA He knows how to get the sound, and he knows how to get up a good earphone mix, which is critical when you're playing like this, everybody live.

Do you try to separate the instruments?

GRISMAN Yeah. We do a certain amount. We have baffles, and there's good enough separation that we can replace parts if we need to. I tend to try to edit around that stuff.

GARCIA It's actually good enough where in one situation I was able to replace a vocal, even though I sing and play guitar at the same time. There was little enough vocal leakage onto the guitar mic. It's difficult [to get that good separation]. It's an amazingly good little room for recording.

GRISMAN When you have your own place, it's like your laboratory. You can experiment with it. No matter how much you rent a studio, very few people will really go in there and spend two days experimenting. When I built this, we spent a day trying to find the right place in the room to put the bass. And since most of what I do is the same kind of instruments, now I have places [figured out].

GARCIA It's good, it's reliable, and it's amazingly consistent, which is the bugaboo of all studios. Consistency is mighty hard to come by. David's choice of microphones is also really well matched.

What are you using?

WHAT THEY PLAY (GARCIA, 1993)

Jerry Garcia played mostly vintage acoustic guitars on *Not for Kids Only,* his collaboration with David Grisman. These instruments include a '39 Gibson Super 400N—natural finish—archtop (Grisman, an avid collector, notes that only a handful of these instruments were made), a Martin D-18 owned by Monroe Grisman (David's son), and Garcia's own D-28. At the *Kids* sessions, these guitars were recorded with Neumann U-89 and KM-85 microphones.

Garcia also records with his Alvarez cutaway acoustic, which he endorses and plays on stage. "It's very balanced," says Garcia. "It's not a powerhouse guitar; it's pretty quiet, but it's got a nice tone. It's acceptable. It just doesn't have the refinement that some of these [vintage] instruments have; some of these have depth, character." For amplification, the Alvarez has a bridge pickup and an internal microphone.

Garcia uses D'Addario strings on his acoustic guitars. "I've been going from lighter to heavier—although the heaviest I use are probably light or light mediums," Garcia says. "If the tune wants a lot of tricky playing, I prefer something lighter and more articulate, because I simply don't have the chops to crunch down real heavy strings with an action that will let me get a big note out of it. I can get a pretty pure note with lighter strings and a slightly lighter touch."

For performance, Garcia favors a generalized approach to string gauge and setup, so that the guitar will be usable for all the different styles he plays in. No matter what the style, though, he stresses the importance of finding the right touch. "On the guitar, if you try to play too loud, you overplay the thing and you get less sound."

For fingerstyle playing, Garcia uses his bare fingers. "It's because that's what I heard on the records, like Mississippi John Hurt and Elizabeth Cotten," he says. "I liked that quiet, first-position sound, the intricate Carolina style of fingerpicking. It takes a lot of time to get a sound with picks on an acoustic guitar. Jorma [Kaukonen] probably gets as good a sound as anybody, a good variety of tone with not too much clatter." As for flatpicks, Garcia likes them very heavy and completely inflexible, with a traditional point.

GRISMAN I use a lot of [Neumann] KM-84s. For Jerry I think we brought in a U-89 and a U-87. Basically, there's not a lot of experimenting. I've got the microphones that I use for what I do, and if somebody requests another microphone or something special, we get one in here.

GARCIA It's nice, because you can focus on the music, not on the sound. You don't have to spend half the day getting a sound, and then by the time you get a sound you're exhausted, you're burned out, and your ears are tired.

I've never had a problem in here. Every time, we just tune up the instruments, go in there, and play it. That's it; we're rolling.

What other collaborations are coming up?

GARCIA Who knows? We have an infinite number of possible things to try.

Anything more that's recorded already that you want to put out?

GRISMAN We have a lot of stuff that's recorded. We were making a *Garcia/Grisman II,* and we had a lot of material and basically we thought we should record it all over again.

GARCIA And somewhere along the line the idea for a children's record popped up.

GRISMAN I like concept albums. One of the things I want to do with this label is not necessarily just have artists who record once a year. I like to make records with some kind of point of view. I'd like to do a jazz record.

I think he should do a bluegrass album, just 'cause he'd enjoy it and I think he has a contribution to make. He's got a natural voice for that kind of music, and he's got enough age on him that it's soulful. [*Garcia laughs.*]

Basically, whatever he wants to do and has time for, I'm into.

GARCIA We have a certain body of material that we have access to. An album of Gershwin tunes, for instance. There are so many things—we could be knocking them out one a year until doomsday.

Emily Saliers (left)
and Amy Ray.

INDIGO GIRLS

Since their debut in the mid-'80s, the high-powered duo known as Indigo Girls has grown from a grass-roots acoustic act to a headliner at the Lilith Fair and arenas packed with some of today's most ardent fans, while their music has broadened from more conventional folk-rock fare to a multi-instrumental, genre-hopping style. At the time of this interview in 1997, the duo—Amy Ray and Emily Saliers—had just released their hardest-hitting record yet, *Shaming of the Sun,* and although they announced in very definite terms on stage that night that their next project was going to be straight acoustic, they instead upped the volume ante even more with 1999's *Come On Now Social,* which included contributions from Sheryl Crow, Joan Osborne, Me'Shell Ndegeocello, and many others. So goes the songwriter's life: you have to follow where the songs want to go.

In person, Ray and Saliers spoke cautiously and concisely, allowing each other plenty of room to offer a contrasting perspective—

just as they do in their music. Interestingly, after all the years of working together, they were discovering basic things about each other's songwriting methods even during this conversation.

NO BOUNDARIES

Warning: the Indigo Girls' album *Shaming of the Sun* is not for purists of any stripe. There's way too much voltage in it for the acoustic-only set, and too much acoustic stuff for people who like their music purely plugged. Not only are all manner of acoustic and electric guitars freely mixed and matched, but bouzouki and banjo sidle up to crunching power chords, electric baritone meets classical guitar, and hurdy-gurdy mingles with piano. The album, which marks the first time the Girls have taken the producer's helm, is a kind of studio free-for-all, with the adventurous arrangements matched by a particularly wide range of moods in the songwriting. Except for a few small missteps—some out-of-place garage guitar, an odd, lumbering horn chart—the whole disc is a blast of fresh writing, fresh playing, and kinetic energy.

Striking contrasts are, of course, nothing new for the Indigo Girls. Their greatest strength has always been the interplay between Amy Ray's primal rock 'n' roll and Emily Saliers' softer, more reflective style. Because they've almost never written together and they contribute equally to the duo's repertoire, Ray and Saliers carry audiences from smoothly crafted folk-pop to angry, cathartic rock to wistful balladry and back again. As radical as *Shaming of the Sun* seems compared to their previous albums, it simply extends the Indigo Girls' natural dynamics into a full studio soundscape.

In April 1997, Ray and Saliers toured briefly as a duo to promote the impending release of *Shaming*, their first collection of new material since

1994's *Swamp Ophelia*. In San Francisco, they previewed eight songs for a packed crowd at the roots-rock club Slim's and met with me backstage to talk about their ever-expanding universe of music.

Tell me about the explosion of stringed instruments on Shaming of the Sun. *Did that happen as a result of experimenting in your writing or because you were trying to broaden the sound for the record?*

SALIERS It was both. For instance, "Get Out the Map" is a song I play banjo on, and I wrote it on banjo. But Amy wrote "Shame on You," and I played banjo on parts of it just for a different color. "Caramia" is the first song I've written on electric guitar. And then other instruments got added to other songs. Bouzouki got added for texture.

RAY Bouzouki got sort of thrown in on the last couple of records. It's one of those things where there's a sound that you're always looking for—it's usually the bouzouki.

SALIERS Cool sound. Very cool sound.

RAY Baritone guitar. Baritone guitar is something I've always loved. We just never had one, but Emily gave me one.

SALIERS We're both trying to grow.

Emily, have you been playing banjo for a long time?

SALIERS No. Amy gave me that banjo years and years ago. I'm not really a banjo player. I can pick out basic chords, and I know how to fingerpick on the guitar, so I just transfer the technique over to the banjo. So I can get away with the cool sound of it without being a good player.

The record has some pretty unusual combinations of banjo with distorted electric guitar.

RAY Banjo is kind of like the ultimate punk instrument, I think. It's got that sound that makes you feel things. It's this cranky old sound. I personally prefer using banjos in a weird way—sort of a perverse Dixieland sound, like a Dixieland march in slow motion.

I've heard a lot of subversive sort of art bands in Atlanta recently, and a lot of them use banjos. It's the new thing that a lot of bands are turning to. It's the Salvation Army sound.

Amy, you were just picking on a mandolin a few minutes ago. Are you playing that much now?

RAY I picked up mandolin just because I've always thought it was fun to play on. I started learning a couple of songs here and there, and then I decided to play "Get Out the Map" on it. Before, I just did "Closer to Fine." But at home I play it just to mess around, just to have a different musical inspiration. All I do is play chords.

Do you have a hard time going between the guitar's tuning in fourths and the fifths on these other instruments, like bouzouki and mandolin?

RAY The mandolin is an upside-down guitar, really, so it's easy to think of it that way—you think of things in terms of patterns, not musically. What do you think, Emily?

SALIERS I've never thought about that, so obviously it's not a big issue. You just find whatever sounds good. Like on a banjo, I can find the major chords within a key. And then I land on other stuff by accident, but I don't really compare it to guitar fingering. I tune the bouzouki any way I want to anyway; I don't do a standard tuning. It's like, "OK, let's get a drony A sounding bouzouki tuning." Kind of like no rules, which is the best way to get good stuff out of instruments that you're not good at.

Do you find that a new instrument leads you into different songwriting territory than you would get to otherwise?

SALIERS I think so. Although today we did a radio interview, and we were playing the song "Get Out the Map," which I wrote on banjo. I played it on guitar because I didn't have a banjo in the studio, and I realized that the chords are just like "Closer to Fine," so I guess that kind of blows that theory. I thought I'd written something different from that.

RAY Yeah, but what you did is write "Get Out the Map," whereas if you'd written it on guitar, you would have gone, "This sounds like 'Closer to Fine,'" and you would have never written the song.

SALIERS It's true.

When you are getting ready to record, do you work your songs out as a duo before going into the studio and adding other instruments?

RAY Yeah. We work out an arrangement that we can play as a duo for most of them. [For *Shaming*] we didn't have some songs quite finished yet, so we went to the studio and jammed on them and finished them. Some of them we didn't have time to arrange, so we arranged them in the studio. But normally we try to do the arrangements so we can play them by ourselves.

This record was different though. As we were arranging, we already had ideas about, "I'm going to play this guitar part, and we'll overdub 12-string with that. . . ." So we were thinking about it the whole time.

Did you know while you were writing that you were going to produce the record?

RAY No. But we always have had something to do with it. No one tells us what to do. Peter [Collins] carried the load of responsibility for us as a producer for the last couple of records, and he's got a great vision, but it was always a team [effort].

This time we didn't know we were going to produce it until a lot of the producers we were asking fell through, and it just came upon the fact that we were going to do it ourselves. And then it really got wide open after that. We just spent a lot of time playing a lot of guitars. It's like the guitar record for us.

How was the recording process different without another person to bounce stuff off of?

SALIERS You have no one to rely on but yourself—although we did work with Dave Leonard. He coproduced it with us, and we worked really well with him. But it still felt like everything was on our shoulders in a way that it hadn't quite been before, which is good. There was a lot more experimentation, freedom to go, "I think I'm just going to try this little part, maybe I'll try this amp, maybe we'll stick hurdy-gurdy on that song," much more of the kitchen-sink mentality, which is really fun. Whereas maybe Peter is less inclined that way.

When you're recording with a lot of instruments and multitracking, how do you maintain a live feel?

RAY The majority of the song is done live. With "Scooter Boys," the whole song's live—no overdubs except for one guitar. And then a song like "Caramia" was cut live and then we went back in and fixed the guitar. You have to pay attention to [the live feel] the whole time so you don't lose it. Part of it is being spontaneous when you're overdubbing—overdubbing inside the control room where the mic is picking up what's coming off the speakers, things that enhance a live feel to the tracks that you're putting down on top of everything. And then not getting so precious about every little thing really helps.

Not worrying about mistakes?

RAY We worry about them, but we embrace them, too.

But you initially record the core instruments all at the same time?

RAY Most of them. The song "Shed Your Skin" was built from the bottom up [from a drum loop]. That was the whole purpose of the song.

Will it be especially hard to translate these album arrangements back to the band for touring?

SALIERS I think we're going to be able to capture the core of the songs fairly well, with [drummer] Jerry [Marotta] and [bassist] Sarah [Lee]. And we're bringing in a new player to do everything we can't do, like violin, or some of the electric guitar parts or acoustic guitar parts—

RAY —or mandolin—

SALIERS —to free us up to do other things. Even with the band, there's stuff that's not going to be able to be captured in exactly the same way. Some tricks we did with percussion, compression, vocal doubling. Sometimes we're going to have to emulate the distance between harmonies physically with the mic rather than [electronically] re-create it.

RAY But if we re-created it totally, it would be boring. That's not what a live show is supposed to be. I'd rather see someone interpret the song a completely different way, because I can go home and listen to the record any time. Emily doesn't always feel the same way.

SALIERS I like a little of both. Sometimes I like the charge of familiarity. "Play that guitar lead like you played on the record." And other times,

"What a great interpretation to do it differently like that." That's why we mix it up.

One of your stylistic trademarks is your vocal arrangements, all that great overlapping and alternating of lines. Where did that idea come from?

SALIERS Sacred music, choir when we were kids. All those counter lines and canons and singing parts that move around each other.

RAY No one was really doing it in the music that we listened to, I don't think. Simon and Garfunkel did, but I didn't listen to that kind of stuff.

We found it was the easiest way for us to work together, [partly] because of weaknesses. I wasn't too good at singing harmony when we first started, so I had to think of it as a melody line. We would be singing opposing melodies, basically. Now I can sing harmony because I've worked on it.

A lot of the stuff we do now grew out of weaknesses—mostly that I had, actually. But it grew into a way that we work together. It ended up being cool, I think. And now we can attain more musically, but we still have that same thing that we always can do.

I was wondering if you were inspired by Joni Mitchell's elaborate vocal arrangements—all those layers of overdubbed voices, like a chorus.

SALIERS I know exactly what you're talking about. She stacked those weird harmonies in the background. They would all sort of move together, the harmony parts, in interesting intervals. 'Cause there's only two of us, until recently we've experimented less with that.

While each of you is writing a song, do you think about what the other might sing?

SALIERS I don't usually think that.

RAY I probably think about it at the end of the writing process, or else I'll have an extra verse, some extra words that I want to use but it's too many words. What I always think is that Emily will just sing it as a countermelody, so that I can still have the lyrics in there. I don't have to have a whole extra verse.

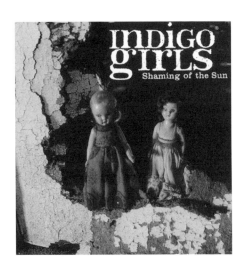

How do you share new songs with each other?

SALIERS Sometimes we'll start songs or be playing them in sound check to test things, just for fun. So I'll start to hear snippets of Amy's ideas early on. By the time she finishes the songs, they'll be somewhat familiar to me. Last time around, I wrote my songs in a pretty short period of time and ended up playing a couple of them for her that I guess she'd never heard even parts of. And it's a loaded moment, you know. You want your partner to like your stuff.

RAY I sang a lot of my new songs in public before I actually played them for her. We had a long time off and we were very separate, and I was doing separate gigs, writer's nights, just to work in new material and figure out if I liked the songs I was writing. Maybe Emily heard something after I'd already played it for an audience, or maybe she was even in the audience and heard it the first time. So that kind of dilutes the loadedness of it a little bit.

Do you ever nix each other's songs or send each other back to the drawing board?

SALIERS No. Not typically at all. Sometimes we'll decide a song is better off if it's a solo song.

RAY Or make suggestions. We'll ask, "What do you think of this?" and the other person might say, "I think the chorus is too long" or "I think we should add a bridge" or "I'm missing this element." If the song's important enough for the person to have written it and believe in it themselves, then you've got to give it a chance.

SALIERS You have to have faith that the process is working, and you have to get used to someone else's ideas being added to your song. You're used to just singing the song alone, and you know it in an intimate and personal way, and then all of a sudden it's become something else. But for the most part, I have faith in the process of what Amy and I have done for so long, and while sometimes it's an adjustment at first, in the end it usually comes out being better.

RAY When I play alone, I tend to be very unstructured. I usually don't have a real definitive tempo. I start and stop and slow down and do things on any given night differently from the night before in the same song. When you play with somebody else, you can't really do that as much. So for me, the songs take on structure, which is good sometimes. But sometimes it's really hard for me to get used to.

Do you record yourself while you're writing?

RAY I do. I tape all the time I'm writing. [*To Emily*] Do you?

SALIERS No. Unless there's a certain thing I want to remember, like a guitar chord progression or a melody line. Then I'll tape it. But usually I'll just write down the notes.

RAY I never listen to tapes when they're done. Ever. I don't know why, but I always tape, 'cause it somehow makes me remember it better.

SALIERS Do you keep them?

RAY Yeah. It's a weird process. I never listen to them.

Do you typically record more material than actually gets on the record?

SALIERS Usually we have just enough.

RAY But we had a lot of songs this time, even ideas for songs. More stuff than we normally write. I had a bunch of songs that I started and put on the back burner because I felt like I already had enough songs for the record. I didn't want to put my energy into finishing them right at that moment; I just wanted to put it into the record. So I've got all those little buds to work on, which is good for me. I usually don't have that many songs. I'm not very prolific. I'm prolific with ideas, but I don't finish them.

Does traveling make it hard to write?

RAY Makes it easier for me.

SALIERS Makes it harder for me, if we're on the road singing. After we play the show, I try to conserve my voice, and when I write I like to sing a lot—sing ideas and try to work stuff out. If we're doing a string of shows, I always think about that, staying up late, stuff like that. So for me, [travel is] more prohibitive, but it's inspiring as far as what you see, what you get to experience. I just have to collect it and do it at a later time.

Both of your guitar styles have evolved quite a bit over the last ten years. How do you think your playing has developed?

RAY Obviously, we use a lot more tunings than we used to. I think all we used when we started was open D. And then Emily would use some Joni Mitchell–type tunings.

SALIERS Mary Chapin Carpenter taught me a couple of tunings, but I didn't start using them until "Galileo"—*Rites of Passage* [*the tuning is D A D G B C, the same as for Carpenter's "The Moon and St. Christopher"*].

RAY And I just turned to tunings as an alternative, you know, to have fun with it. "Center Stage" [from *Indigo Girls*] was in open D. I remember hearing the B-52s, that guy Ricky [Wilson]—he died. He played every song they had in a different tuning. He never played anything in standard tuning, and I just remember thinking about that—it was really inspiring. The guitar became an endless spectrum at that point. I'm not a really good guitar player, so to change tunings opens up new worlds for me.

SALIERS We try to make it as expansive as we possibly can with just the two of us, not just for the sake of being expansive, but because it's more gratifying than, "Let's just play the same chords." Personally, I used to play much more jazz-oriented chords and was really influenced by this local singer-songwriter. And then I found after a while emotionally I just couldn't get as much out of playing that way. In some ways it's a lot easier technically to play in a more aggressive style, and emotionally it's much more accessible.

Are there a lot of open tunings on Shaming of the Sun*?*

RAY Yeah. We're always in different tunings from each other, too. I don't know how that happens.

SALIERS What's that song where you're in D-minor tuning [D A D F A D]?

RAY "Everything in Its Own Time," but I'm actually capoed on the fourth fret, so it would be F♯ minor. I love the open D-minor tuning a lot. It's a great tuning, so I'll just capo and use it for different songs. I discovered it when we were doing a cover of a Vic Chesnutt song called "Free of Hope" and I wanted to play it on slide, so I did it in open D minor and played it on electric guitar.

Emily, how are you tuned on "Everything in Its Own Time"?

SALIERS I'm capoed on the second fret and playing sort of A-minor chords. I'm in standard tuning except for the B string, which is tuned down to A.

RAY Sometimes we come up with all these different tunings that sound good with each other, and then we forget what we've decided. Like in "Scooter Boys," I don't know what tuning you were in . . .

SALIERS E minor.

RAY And I had the [low] E string dropped to D. Our tunings don't match at all for that. There's discord notes all over the place. I had to listen to the tape to figure out what we were doing.

SALIERS There's even parts of that that I can't figure out what I did, 'cause it happened so spur-of-the-moment. I was in E-minor tuning because we were getting ready to work on a different song, and then Amy started jamming on the song and Andy [Stochansky, from Ani DiFranco's band] started playing the drums and Sarah was playing bass. So I said, "Oh well, I don't have time to change my tuning, I'll just stick in this tuning and see what I can find."

RAY She's tuned weird for "Don't Give That Girl a Gun." What do you tune in?

SALIERS It's like an open-D tuning with the A string dropped down [D G D F♯ A D].

"Burn All the Letters" sounds to me like open D.

SALIERS Now that's a weird one because of the key change.

RAY I'm in open E♭

SALIERS I start in open D, so I play the chunka-chunk in the beginning. [When the song modulates to E♭] Amy takes over the chunka-chunk and I play muted a half step up. I obviously can't play open chords.

RAY It was a bitch to do, but it ended up being cool. Guitars take on a different character when you tune them differently. The minor tunings are really sad and beautiful.

All these tunings must explain why you have so many guitars on stage.

RAY Yeah, we feel gluttonous sometimes, but we are in different tunings from each other on most songs, or different capo positions at least. And then, there are never two songs in a row that are in the same tuning. When we didn't have a tech, we used to have to arrange our set list so that we did every song with a capo on the third fret in a row.

SALIERS I can't believe we ever did that.

RAY We didn't arrange it by what sounded best, but by what was the easiest to keep in tune.

Are you playing more electric now than you used to?

SALIERS Yeah, definitely. That's a totally different field from acoustic, obviously. It's getting used to [the instrument], and then it's like a whole world of choices, not only among different amps, but on that one amp, you know, how you set it, the EQ, what pedals you're going to use, or what tone knobs you're going to use on your guitar. There are so many variables. It's like learning a whole other instrument.

RAY A lot of our songs translate. I write a lot of songs on electric that I end up playing on acoustic. I just write on electric because I have a particular amp in a particular room at my house, and I like the way it sounds. When I feel inspired, I write on that instead of acoustic.

One of the things I enjoy about the way you play acoustic is that you show it off as a real rock instrument rather than the typical way that rock musicians use it, for accompanying slow ballads. The acoustic rhythm part on "Scooter Boys" is about as rocking as it could be, and I think it rocks harder than it would have if you had played it on an electric guitar.

RAY I agree. I listen to much more electric than I do acoustic music, but I prefer most of the time playing acoustic guitar. I just get more rock out of it. I love the noise on it. What I like about electric is turning the reverb up and doing things that are esoteric, Neil Young-y, like the sound track for *Dead Man,* that kind of sound.

In a way, your acoustic style goes back to those early rock records by bands like the Rolling Stones and the Who. There's lots of acoustic guitar on those records, but most people don't really think of them that way.

RAY It's the combo. It's the electric with the acoustic that really works for me. The acoustic gives you that edge that the electric can't give you sometimes, that rhythm, that percussion where you can feel it, but then the electric bites. It's good, because Emily can do all the electric parts—

SALIERS Learning!

RAY —and I'll just play the acoustic.

The acoustic guitars you play on stage—almost all Martins—are really varied in size. Is that for sonic variety?

RAY There are certain guitars that sound better on certain songs for me, like my little 0. My

SELECTED DISCOGRAPHY

Come On Now Social, Epic 69914 (1999).
Shaming of the Sun, Epic 67891 (1997).
1200 Curfews, Epic 67229 (1995).
Swamp Ophelia, Epic 57621 (1994).
Rites of Passage, Epic 48865 (1992).
Nomads, Indians, Saints, Epic 46820 (1990).
Indigo Girls, Epic 45044 (1989).
Strange Fire, Epic 45427 (originally released 1987).

WHAT THEY PLAY (1997)

Indigo Girls Emily Saliers and Amy Ray play a battery of Martin guitars. Ray's main ones are an O-18, a black J-40M, a D-35, and a J-40 12-string. "I've never found anything that sounded better," says Ray. "I've played everything. I'll hear Bruce Springsteen play a Takamine, and I'll go, 'Oh my God, I want to sound like that,' and then I'll play it and it doesn't sound as good. I play so hard. Martins are great 'cause they're bluegrass instruments and you can bang on them." Like most bluegrass players, she uses medium-gauge strings—a Martin set. Ray also has several guitars made by Atlanta luthier Kent Everett, including a 12-string and two six-strings, one of which she uses on stage as a high-string guitar (with the bottom four strings tuned an octave higher than usual) for the song "Mystery." "His guitars sound the best of the guitars that I've heard high-strung," she says. "I love the sound of a high-strung guitar, but it's the kind of thing that you don't want to overuse."

Saliers' main acoustics are a Brazilian rosewood D-35, a rare koa D-45, and a J-40, all strung with D'Addario lights. She also plays an Alvarez-Yairi classical and a wood-bodied Dobro (which she used on "This Train Revised" from *Swamp Ophelia*). For electrics, she plays a mid-'60s Stratocaster and an "old, cheesy" National through either a Vox AC-30 reissue or a Peavey 50 Classic with two 12-inch speakers.

Both Saliers and Ray use Shubb capos and Dunlop Tortex picks. Saliers also uses a thumbpick for banjo and nylon-string guitar along with her bare fingers. "I've never gotten quite used to [fingerpicks]," she says. "They make your fingers feel disconnected from what's going on." Using bare fingers also allows her to switch easily from fingerpicking to strumming, as she often does in midsong.

Ray and Saliers use L.R. Baggs pickups and TC Electronic preamps for the amplification of all their acoustics except Saliers' Dobro, which has a Highlander pickup. "We're picky, picky," says Ray. "I mean, I can hear a string imbalance in the middle of a crowded bar. It's important to me. The guitar has to be an extension of you in order to perform with it, so it's got to sound great. It can sound great in a crappy bar or a big room. It's not [about having] the most expensive equipment; it's just that your guitar has to feel like you." They use no other effects on their acoustics, except when Saliers switches to an amp sound for an occasional slide break.

Clearly Ray and Saliers are tone fanatics, although they don't consider themselves true gearheads. "We're not equipment goobers," Ray says, "but there's nothing wrong with equipment goobers. Some of my best friends are."

little 0 is a great studio guitar. It's the one I've had the longest, and I love that guitar. My J-40 is good for very full, loud songs, and I find the D-35's are good for stuff where you need a little warmth. You can pick, and with kind of soft strumming, they always sound really full but present, too.

Emily, do you have similar kinds of divisions of labor for your guitars?

SALIERS For acoustic guitar, I have mainly two that I use. The D-45's a little lighter, a little crispier, and it's really good for picking; and the J-40, I get a little more meat out of. On certain songs, maybe someone in the audience couldn't tell if I'm playing one or the other, like "Galileo," but to me, "Galileo" feels just so natural on that D 45, and when I play it on the other one, it just feels weird. Sonically, I can tell the difference.

Hearing your cover of "Down by the River" earlier tonight reminded me of Neil Young and the way he's drawn to extremes. It seems like there's a connection to what you're doing. Do you feel that at all?

RAY He's one of my favorites of all time. He's my main man. Definitely. We're drawn to extremes.

So many musicians struggle with the labeling of their music: I'm playing an acoustic guitar, and that means that I'm a folkie, but I don't want to be a folkie because it's not commercial. You seem liberated from that whole game somehow.

RAY That's good.

SALIERS Certain things can be frustrating—radio formats that decide they don't want to even listen to your music to see if they want to play it, because they've already decided what your music is like. It would be great to have radio stations that just played all kinds of stuff, break down all those barriers. But I'd say for the most part we are unaffected by all that stuff.

I don't think we set up any boundaries for ourselves as far as what we want to try or how we want to play. Whatever we feel compelled to do, that's what we do, even if it's a disaster.

CHRIS WHITLEY

Chris Whitley is one of contemporary rock's true rebel poets, a visionary songwriter whose sounds and images get under your skin. He had a moment in the national-media spotlight with the release of his debut album, *Living with the Law,* but his restless explorations proved to be too rough and unpredictable for the mainstream rock world. The experience of rise and fall in the music industry proves wrenching for many artists, and at the time of this conversation in 1998, Whitley was just beginning to feel at home again with his music and with his relatively small but rabidly devoted audience (on the particular night of this interview, the sardine-packed crowd included at least one young man dressed in Whitley's stage uniform of boots, jeans, white tank top, and bowler hat). Among musicians, Whitley stirs deep passions; of all my published interviews (many with much more famous names), only the piece on Joni Mitchell inspired more reader mail and commentary.

In the years since our conversation, Whitley has continued his creative stride, touring with such artists as Alanis Morissette and Jonny Lang and releasing two albums in 2000: *Live at Martyrs,* which captures the gutbucket intensity of his solo shows, and *Perfect World,* a sublime collection of rock and blues covers performed with Billy Martin and Chris Wood of the jazz-jam trio Medeski Martin and Wood.

GRIT AND GROOVE

Some of the world's coolest music happens when instruments fall into the hands of people who don't know—or don't care—what they're *supposed* to do with them. The guy on stage at the San Francisco club Bottom of the Hill wears a bowler hat and picks a battered old National guitar. He's a bluesman, right? That's what people *do* with guitars like these. Well, not exactly. He's got a magnetic pickup on the scraped-up top of his National, and on some songs he cranks up a heavy rock sound through his amp that would make most country blues fans dive for cover. Deeper into his set, he sings softly and sweetly and plays chromatic harmonies like a bebop balladeer. In other songs, he's a grooving soul singer, a twisted banjo frailer, and some sort of—yes—primal bluesman playing noisy slide with a piece of bicycle handlebar.

The musician in question, Chris Whitley, is one of the most original and enigmatic new singer-songwriter voices of the '90s, and he's just released an acoustic masterpiece called *Dirt Floor.* Recorded live in one day with one microphone in a barn in Vermont—just Whitley's voice, guitar and banjo, and foot stomps—*Dirt Floor* is a stunning portrait of his visceral, poetic music. It's a record that many fans have been waiting for ever since Whitley's 1991 Columbia debut, *Living with the Law*, introduced a potent blend of National guitar, R&B-inspired vocals, and a gravelly rock band. Subsequent albums *Din of Ecstasy* and *Terra Incognita* carried Whitley further into electric atmospheres, bearing the unmistakable mark of producer Daniel Lanois (Emmylou Harris' *Wrecking Ball*, Bob Dylan's *Time Out of Mind*) and kindred spirit Malcolm Burn. Those albums also carried Whitley way out of the mainstream and into a commercial netherland that made him question his talents and future. When his major-label run inevitably ended, he revived himself creatively and spiritually with the no-budget, no-expectations *Dirt Floor*, which equals if not surpasses his debut.

For someone whose music can be so brawny and intense, Whitley in person is disarmingly soft-spoken and gentle, polite to the point of being downright old-fashioned. (Appearances deceive: even the tattoos on his arms turn out to be based on drawings by his daughter, not some mark of machismo.) Before his packed performance at Bottom of the Hill, he sat down with me at a nearby café to put away several double espressos and retrace the surprising routes of his life and music.

What was your first encounter with a National guitar?

WHITLEY It was the song "Dallas," on Johnny Winter's first major record [*Johnny Winter*, 1969]. It was just a solo acoustic Delta blues on a record that's psychedelic blues-rock, sort of a power trio. He was like the next Hendrix in that period. He was great. I haven't really listened to him since then. But I liked the sound of the National, and it seemed cool.

I played electric guitar when I first was starting in high school, and I played a gig and hated it. I had big amps and all this shit, I couldn't really play at all, and it was really bad. I sold everything I had and bought a National. Someone had just showed me an open tuning, and it kind of fell into my hands—playing slide and that sort of thing.

[Playing a National] was pragmatic too. The National is loud. That's the original reason why guys used them, street guys, 'cause they were louder. I grew up playing on the street too.

What other acoustic guitar music inspired you at the time?

WHITLEY I always [was attracted to] the rude side of rock guitar—I didn't feel like a strumming folk guy, really, though I grew up on enough Dylan. I've always loved that. I loved Dylan's guitar playing back then, too, his early *Times They Are a-Changing, Another Side of Bob Dylan*. . . . But a lot

of my attraction to acoustic guitar as a rock instrument was like *Zeppelin 3,* probably, or *Hunky Dory* from Bowie, or even *Every Picture Tells a Story,* from Rod Stewart—that blend of stuff, electric and acoustic.

So you weren't listening to a lot of music that featured resonator guitars in particular.

WHITLEY No. I was listening to none really, and I'm sure that has affected my [style]. I started to realize in the early '80s or late '70s that I was getting very staccato in my picking. And it was really because I was very into Gary Numan. I was hearing a lot of sequencer, rigid-sounding music that to me was coldly emotional—it's a bit melodramatic, of course, but there's something earnest in it too that's soulful. I think I was trying to play something like what I was hearing. And then I got into playing syncopated, probably from Earth, Wind, and Fire's horn section and James Brown and Prince and other stuff that wasn't really blues rhythmically.

When you listen to old, really cool [blues], a lot of it is pretty close to jazz. It's just about expression, and the form is not really fixed. Early '50s and back—that's about the only period of blues that really gets me, the most rural stuff or the early electric. Early Howlin' Wolf, early '40s John Lee Hooker, stuff like that.

Were slide tunings like open G [D G D G B D] part of your playing right from the start?

WHITLEY I played open G for ten years or so. Except for open E, all the other tunings I've used I've just made up. They're probably in a book; they could be standard tunings for all I know, but I just came up with them in trying to throw myself off.

I started playing in open tunings after I'd been playing guitar for about a year. I was sort of refusing to learn how to play—I never took any lessons—and it was a kind of rebellious or insecure thing for me.

A lot of the tunings listed on your Web site [www.chriswhitley.com] look like you've taken an open-A or open-E tuning and started fiddling with it a bit. Is that something you consciously do?

WHITLEY No. Sometimes I've mistuned something . . . I try to throw myself out of habits. I have a lot of habits because I'm really a limited guitarist, and I learned to play from writing songs.

That's very similar to how Joni Mitchell describes her tuning experiments. Even the kinds of things you do on guitar—a lot of harmonic movement, combinations of open strings with notes fretted up high—remind me of her style, even though the music itself sounds totally different.

WHITLEY That's true. I was listening to her when *Blue* first came out, and *Ladies of the Canyon,* when I lived in Mexico with my mom—the records that are really sparse instrumentation, like just cello and guitar, produced by her. I didn't know then that she was playing open tunings; I knew Jimmy Page did, and he fingerpicked.

A lot of Jimmy Page's acoustic stuff was inspired by her, from what I understand.

WHITLEY There are people that I don't think of often who really affected me on some level. . . . It pisses me off that when my first record came out, it was probably because the Robert Johnson set came out that same year, and on Columbia, they kind of marketed me the best way they could figure out to [as a bluesman]. And I am bluesy, but they made a big deal out of the open tunings, and it was like, "This has been going on forever." I'm certainly not the first person to play steel guitar on a popish song.

When you're playing, are you at all aware of what notes you're tuned to or what chords you're playing?

WHITLEY The only thing I'm aware of is how it relates to my vocal range. I've only become aware of that in the last eight years or something.

I think that I have an analytical enough head, but what I need from music is not very cerebral. There's a degree of me that I try to keep a little naive, for good or bad. I did go through a period of trying to learn how to sight-read and stuff. I gave up, and maybe it was a matter of discipline, or maybe it wasn't what I need from music. It didn't motivate me to learn music mathematically. My favorite shit, in writing words too, is when I don't have an idea and it's more instinctive or subconscious. You just let it go.

A lot of people who play in open tunings are really seduced by the open strings, to the point where they're kind of stuck on them. But in a song like

"From One Island to Another" from Dirt Floor, *the chords move in a jazzy way that the guitar is clearly not dictating through the tuning. You're working the tuning like a composer.*

WHITLEY That song reminded me of my second record, *Din*. It's a jazz thing that I really like that's hard. That's one of my favorite songs on the record. I wanted to write something like a Nat King Cole song, like a jazz ballad, that would sound great if it was just piano and voice, or piano, strings, and voice. I was scared a little bit when I first wrote it that I was being a little too [*pauses*] colorful or something. I hear those kinds of changes, the half steps and this kind of thing, a lot, but I try to avoid them because I think I might alienate people or be guitar-indulgent. Then again, I hear Thelonious Monk do solo piano, and I really don't need much more music than that. I love that clumsy-ass but really expressive thing about him. It's very sophisticated but very primitive at the same time.

There's something, too, in the pentatonic droniness of blues that's primitive. I'm listening to Indonesian and Vietnamese music lately, and it's mostly pentatonic and around one key. Indian, Egyptian music, it's all related. I think it's timeless music. I feel sometimes that harmony is more European and more cerebral than where we started from—vocal things and drums. I still do like the droney thing a lot, but I know what you mean, I sometimes get really annoyed with that.

Somehow, the sound of the National in combination with the tunings puts an entirely different spin on those jazz chords.

WHITLEY With something like "Island," if I played those same voicings in standard tuning or on an electric guitar, they'd get Holiday Inn–ish to me. Even playing the same thing [up and down the neck] with all the same open strings, or changing one note in a chord progression, using it almost as part of a progression: I don't think I would have gotten into that if I played standard, because there are more possibilities [with an open tuning].

I love the banjo sound of "Ball Peen Hammer," in that minor tuning. It's pretty spooky.

WHITLEY Kind of Bill Withers playing banjo [*laughs*]. I always loved the sound of frailing, and I did a song on my last record that I wrote on a banjo ["Still Point," on *Terra Incognita*]. I always thought a groove song would be easy as hell on a banjo. I had a funk band in Europe when I lived there, and I played in some electro-pop bands. I was always into that one-chord

stuff you can do—it's very close to blues. Prince is great with that, and Cameo is great with that, and a lot of ethnic music. I thought, "Learn how to frail." Not bluegrass, but just funky, dumb-ass banjo, very crude kind of playing. And when I was coming up with that song, I realized that I don't want to hear frailing out of my own hands. So I just gave up and came up with my own thing. It's still very undeveloped.

Are you playing with your fingers?

WHITLEY I use a flatpick and two fingerpicks and I pull with my fist, which you don't do on frailing. I like that sound rhythmically; it's a little bit swing or upbeat or something. It's kind of like an Elmore James riff.

On Dirt Floor, *the title of the song "Scrapyard Lullaby" is so evocative. When you're writing lyrics, does an image or phrase like this take hold and lead you into the song?*

WHITLEY Yeah. I came up with that title before the tune. I often feel most fulfilled by my own things when I don't know what I'm writing about at

first. I just get something that I believe in enough to sing to and mumble into a Walkman and try to listen back without deliberating words. And then I start getting an idea. It comes around to making beautiful stuff out of junk, out of nothing, something Zen-ish. I didn't know exactly what I was getting at with "Scrapyard Lullaby." I just liked the title. I do edit lyrics a lot to try to articulate to someone else—not just to be more popular, but to be more accessible, where I'm not just indulging myself. Because writing is really a selfish thing for me. I do it because I need to, but I do have a need for it to have some resonance for other people.

What inspired you to record Dirt Floor *the way you did—straight live, acoustic, and solo?*

WHITLEY When I was on Sony Records, I had gotten really anxious about being on the radio and where I fit in. I don't fit in anywhere that easily, but I think I fill a void—maybe I do. I'd been doubting everything that I'd been doing. I'd been touring, and I hadn't been writing. The week I got off Sony I started writing again, and then I decided to do something solo. I had this Web site a man in Alabama started on his own, and 10,000 people subscribed to it. I thought, I'll just make something and maybe they'll like it. Just trying to encourage myself to get past worrying about "my place in the record industry." Living in New York is part of that too: it's very media driven and you're either hip or not, and I've never been exactly hip in that *Spin* magazine way, in an MTV way, just kind of mainstream hip [*laughs*]. But it doesn't appeal to me much.

So I just encouraged myself to write, and over a two-month period I basically wrote some songs. I had given up the funk band I had and was trying to write what I was feeling. I didn't think about whether there was a chorus or not or a hook or not. I didn't have the confidence at the time to even know whether I could stand what I was writing: "I can't record this." So I played it for [producer] Craig Street. Craig did k.d. lang's last record [*Drag*]. He did two Cassandra Wilson records that he had me play on [*Blue Light 'til Dawn* and *New Moon Daughter*]. He's done a bunch of records since. He's a great guy. He's got a strange background—quite a mix of tastes, from Duke Ellington and old blues and old jazz to crude-ass blues, and he kind of sees it all in a similar way to world music. He can hear music in something real clumsy, where a lot of people want to shine it up. But I trust Craig. I played him stuff, and he said, "Man, it's great. Don't think about it anymore. Write another tune."

Even when we went to record, he'd say, "No, we got five takes. Let's go on to the next thing. We're leaving tomorrow. You've got to finish this instead of picking over each thing." So that's how it evolved. I originally started with the idea of doing it on a DAT at home in my apartment in New York—cars going by in the background or whatever, funky as hell—and putting it out over a Web site. Then I started realizing I didn't have the money to pay for the manufacturing, and I was thinking about the administration, like who's gonna deal with publishers and ASCAP and everything. And a friend of mine [Brandon Kessler of Messenger Records] has put out a lot of records with this other friend of mine. He used to be an intern at Sony. He was into doing it. It cost nothing. It cost like renting the van. Everybody did it for free. Craig did it for nothing. My friend Danny Kadar engineered it. We did it on one microphone.

Was it a vintage mic?

WHITLEY No, it's a Speiden stereo ribbon mic. It's made out of a gun barrel. It's a very small company, and they don't make mics anymore. We used two mic pres [preamps], left and right, that an English guy makes mostly for people who are recording classical records, for acoustic recording. And Danny had a 1965 Ampex quarter-inch two-track—you know, a mastering machine—and we just went live to that in a little room where I used to work on motorcycles in this barn at this house my dad owns that no one lives in anymore. It was free to go up there. We just did it. I meant it to come out even faster. It became more of a wait than I wanted originally, but it was much less than a large label would have done if they'd invested money. Brandon was excited about it, so he just did all that he could and got a publicity company involved. It took on a different dimension than what I expected.

So you just adjusted the mic to get the voice and guitar balanced?

WHITLEY They were in the kitchen and I was in the barn. There's a little hallway in between,

DISCOGRAPHY

Perfect World, Valley Entertainment 15119 (2000).

Live at Martyrs, Messenger 07 (2000). Messenger, PO Box 1607, New York, NY 10113; www.messengerrecords.com.

Dirt Floor, Messenger 04 (1998).

Terra Incognita, Work/Sony OK 67507 (1996).

Din of Ecstacy, Work/Sony 52970 (1995).

Living with the Law, Columbia CK 46966 (1991).

STREET WISE

"I think there's a power to acoustic instruments that gets ignored a lot, so it's a texture that I go to a lot," says producer extraordinaire Craig Street, who has presided over such acoustic masterworks as Cassandra Wilson's *Blue Light 'til Dawn* and *New Moon Daughter* and Chris Whitley's *Dirt Floor*. "With Cassandra I thought that if those textures were in there, they wouldn't be typical of someone who's perceived as being jazz. In other instances, whether it's with k.d. [lang] or Holly [Cole] or Jeb [Loy Nichols], I've been into flipping the textures: hearing the electric instruments as the background instruments and hearing the acoustic instruments a little more in the foreground."

In the case of *Dirt Floor*, Street used a single ribbon mic to capture the unalloyed sound of a "guy in a room with a guitar"—like Robert Johnson's hotel room sessions or Nick Drake's *Pink Moon*—and spotlight Whitley's exceptional songwriting. "Ribbons tend to be really natural with acoustic instruments—with all kinds of instruments," Street says. "I use them on electric guitars, I use them on drums, I use them on everything, practically, because they're not hyped up. I think we're really used to hearing how hyped-up something is when you use a really great condenser mic."

That philosophy extends past the individual instrument sounds to the recording as a whole. "You don't have to make records that are complete structures," Street says. "You can let people use their imaginations for what might be there. It's great sometimes when you think you hear something in a piece of recorded music, but it's just your brain filling in what you want to be there at a particular point in time. [In the recording process] that's always a good point to stop."

and you can close the doors. We brought up an amp and some speakers, and we hung the mic from a wire in the ceiling. It made me feel like if I get into another record deal, which I'll probably do, I'd like to do one record like this a year. I just think it's organic, it's nurturing. It's not a big deal; there's no big money involved. It can just be what it is. It doesn't need to have hype. Either you like it or you don't. It's purer that way.

I think that would be healthy for produced records of mine, too. That's kind of how Craig approaches stuff. Daniel Lanois is similar in approach; he'll get more into sound processing, but basically it's how the musicians feel while they're playing that you're hoping to get on the record.

Even mixing—Mark Howard, who coproduced my last record and engineered my first one with me (Mark did the *Sling Blade* sound track with Dan, the Emmylou record, the Dylan record)—Mark does performance mixes. They don't use automated boards. They do a bunch of mixes, and however Mark is feeling is how the mix is gonna be. And some shit'll be too loud. They're more reactive than deliberated over. It's a value statement, which is really hard in the music industry now, because it's such an *industry.*

It's great to hear your guitar work so clearly on Dirt Floor. *What sort of slide do you use to get such a gritty sound?*

WHITLEY It's a short piece of bicycle handlebar. This one [*takes it out of a small leather sack*] I made in New Orleans five years ago. But I made that design 15 years ago when I was playing in funk bands in Europe and using slide and fingering in the same songs. It's cut off on the top so I can turn it around [and fret with the slide finger]. I patented it. It's not the kind of thing many people would be into. I [slide with] my little finger, and I like a slide to be short because I'm not that clean a player. Glass ones are better, I think, if you play real clean.

I don't like that much honestly horizontal slide playing, and most electric slide guitar doesn't really attract me that much. Muddy Waters or Elmore James, I love it spiritually, but it's not what I want to hear from myself. So when I play electric slide, it's more chaotic and more around one area, on all the strings—long, slow notes. People have asked me to record, and they say, "Do your thing. Play slide." And they want to hear, like, Ry Cooder, and I don't do that. I don't really hear it. I would love to hear slide played in the way of those double-reed Egyptian instruments that follow vocals, or those Chinese instruments that bend strings—with the frets real high. Slide is very akin to that kind of thing.

Do you keep your slide on all the time while you're playing?

WHAT THEY PLAY (1998)

On his solo tour following the release of *Dirt Floor,* Chris Whitley played five of the instruments used on that record: a '31 National Style O, a '31 National Triolian, a '56 National Reso-phonic with an old Danelectro pickup (used on the song "Indian Summer"), a '58 Gibson ES-125 (also used a lot on *Terra Incognita*), and a '95 Bart Reiter five-string banjo. On the album version of "Loco Girl," he played a '36 Gibson L-0. As you might gather from this list, Whitley prefers old instruments—"old stuff that's been played a lot," he says. "I like the sound of it more."

Whitley uses D'Addario strings on all his instruments—nickel-wound electric strings on everything but the Gibson L-0, which has a bronze-wound acoustic set. The gauges vary: the Triolian has stock extra-lights (.011 first string), the Style O and the L-0 have .013 first strings and .022 wound third strings, and the ES-125 has a .012 first string and a .021 third.

The Nationals are outfitted with Barcus-Berry magnetic Dobro pickups, which Whitley runs through a tube DI called the Juice Box (made by Retrospec) and into a Fender Pro Junior amp. "This is different than playing totally acoustic," Whitley says. "I can be more dynamic. I can be quieter and louder. I use a DI and a mic on the amp so I can push it and it'll distort and also be clean enough to articulate."

Whitley plies this arsenal of instruments with a purple Dunlop flatpick and metal fingerpicks on his ring and middle fingers. On his pinky he wears a slide he made from a piece of bicycle handlebar, which is cut so that he can rotate it out of the way for fretting.

Last but not least, in his solo show Whitley stomps out the beat on a boot board that's amplified with a Fishman upright bass transducer.

WHITLEY Some songs, if it's clumsy, I'll stick it in my back pocket. My hand is so used to the weight of it that I almost phrase better with it on, believe it or not.

Before I designed this slide, in the late '70s, I was listening to Hendrix a lot and trying to bend the strings behind the tailpiece on the Dobro! I used to use a thumb ring to pull off of the low strings, and I tried using the ends of cigar tips so I could fret and slide [*laughs*], which never worked. I was really into Hendrix-like experimenting, but on a National. But not like [experimental guitarist] Eugene Chadbourne—I didn't have the technique to be doing that. Just trying to find my own thing. And then playing Dobro through wah-wahs . . .

In the '70s I played solo on Bleecker Street, and I had two amps and I had a transducer under the tailpiece and a [magnetic] pickup—I cut a hole in a Dobro and stuck a pickup in. I couldn't mix between the two, so I just mixed volumes [on the amps], and I was playing electric and acoustic. Now there's a solid-bodied resophonic that the National company makes with a transducer under the bridge and a pickup, and you can mix between the two. It's kind of how I use these now with a DI and a tube amp. The harder you hit it, the more you squash and distort it. With a band I use a volume pedal and just drive the amp harder, and if I back off, it can be semi-clean. So I can sort of get the vibe of both. It's not a pure sound; it's a hybrid.

Lots of guitarists these days are experimenting with electrified acoustic sounds. Among electric guitarists, it seems like the tones have become so standardized.

WHITLEY I find that in rock music in general, I'd rather hear women singing, playing electric guitars, and screaming than guys. I don't need to hear another guy rock band anymore. I love playing electric, but since Hendrix, who cares? When I was first attracted to electric guitar as a kid, it was rebellious—guitar in general was a rebellious thing. Now it's like a tennis racket or a golf club. Back then jocks didn't play guitar. It seems to me now that guys singing sweetly would be more rebellious than guys screaming.

In rock, there's a wall of coolness between the audience and you. In a weird way, [Kurt] Cobain made people notice that. There was obviously a vulnerable side to his screaming; it was more like Howlin' Wolf, more visceral than machismo. I thought about that a lot with this record, and Craig pushed me: "Man, you're always afraid of being sweet or singing quiet or in the low register of your voice." And it encouraged me to be more vulnerable.

Tim Reynolds (left)
and Dave Matthews.

DAVE MATTHEWS
AND TIM REYNOLDS

The rise of the Dave Matthews Band, with its unconventional blend

of acoustic instrumentation with the language of progressive rock

and jazz, was one of the great surprises of the '90s—a classic example

of what can happen when enterprising musicians take their

case directly to the fans rather than relying on industry machinery

to "break" (and mold) them. Alongside the band's relentless touring,

the DMB's front man found time to perform frequently in a

stripped-down acoustic setting with his old pal Tim Reynolds, bringing

a high-wire approach and rock 'n' roll drive to the guitar duo

format. That sound was captured in a double CD recorded live

in 1996 and released in 1999, the year in which this raucous

and funny conversation took place at the last stop of another long

duo tour. For Matthews, these tours with Reynolds were clearly a place to unwind from the complexities and pressures of his band's arena extravaganzas, and to reconnect with his roots as a guitarist and songwriter.

Since this conversation, the Dave Matthews Band went on to release another generous double CD from their concert archives, *Listener Supported,* while working on material for the studio follow-up to *Before These Crowded Streets.* Meanwhile, Tim Reynolds continued his solo acoustic adventures with the CD *See into Your Soul* and a supporting tour in 2000.

BAND IN A BOX

On this crisp spring afternoon outside the Berkeley Community Theater, there's no mistaking the preparations for the ritual called the Big Rock Show. Roadies are unloading a truckful of gear through the closely guarded stage door, and teen- and college-age fans—some of whom have traveled from several states away—are milling around, hoping for a glance, an autograph, or a photo op with the Big Rock Star known as Dave Matthews.

Inside the theater, though, any suggestion of a hyped-up "show" vanishes. On the stage sit only five acoustic guitars, a chair, and a few mics, boxes, and cords. The crew is casual but focused, and when Matthews arrives, he greets everyone with a familial friendliness. With his short hair, athletic frame, cotton sweater, and khakis, he looks less like a rock star than a fraternity brother from up the hill at the University of California. His duo partner, Tim Reynolds, makes quite a contrast—short, wiry, and a bit scraggly, all in black from punker boots on up, he's ready for underground clubbing.

The show tonight marks the end of Matthews' and Reynolds' latest acoustic tour, following the release of their double CD *Live at Luther College,* recorded in 1996. With two acoustic guitars and Matthews' silk-and-sandpaper voice, this duo brings to life the knotty, intense songs that have made the Dave Matthews Band such a compelling and surprising force in contemporary rock. The DMB is emphatically a *band,* democratically balancing acoustic guitar, sax, violin, drums, and bass (the sole electric instrument) in expansive arrangements full of harmonic and rhythmic jags. But it's amazing how much of that richness and variety comes across in these duo shows. It's a testimony to the depth of Matthews' vision as a songwriter and guitarist, and to Reynolds' range as an accompanist, from subtle doubling to delay-based atmospherics to pure shredding.

As Matthews and Reynolds grab guitars and sit down with me to talk and play music, it's immediately clear that despite their surface differences, these are very close friends and partners in crime. Reynolds has played on all the DMB albums and frequently joins the band on stage, in addition to pursuing his own projects in freewheeling solo guitar improv, rock, and funk. In conversation, Reynolds and Matthews feed off each other's kinetic energy and quick humor (sly and urbane one moment, locker-room adolescent the next), and when Matthews starts playing something on guitar, Reynolds locks in with him in a microbeat.

I've heard that you two met when Tim was playing in a bar in Charlottesville, Virginia, and Dave was the bartender. Is that a true story?

MATTHEWS Mmm, sort of. I think we met before I started working at Millers. We lived in the same town, and I love watching music, and Tim was one of the Charlottesville musicians—

REYNOLDS —posers.

MATTHEWS Posers. I just loved Tim's playing, so then we just got to know each other.

The cool thing was that people like Tim had [the trio] TR3: he was doing his solo thing, playing jazz gigs; he had tons of gigs. All the musicians were sort of wrapped up together. Carter [Beauford], who's with [the Dave Matthews Band] on drums, played in Secrets and Tim was playing in Secrets, and they probably crossed paths in a lot of different situations.

And two of the guys who sat in on this last album [*Before These Crowded Streets*] were also old friends of ours from Charlottesville—Greg Howard [Chapman Stick] and John D'earth [string arrangements].

Tim, were you playing free-improv acoustic guitar at that time?

REYNOLDS At that point I was probably doing electric, but that evolved. I did that gig for over ten years. It started out solo electric guitar with effects, and somewhere I started playing sitar and did that for a long time, and then I started playing acoustic.

MATTHEWS Monday night at Millers . . . I remember coming in, it was electric for a while, and then all of a sudden violin, and then all of a sudden cello, and then sitar. And then he'd even play drums for a while—it was cool.

REYNOLDS I learned to play a lot of instruments on this gig. And that kind of led to the acoustic guitar as encompassing all the earlier stuff. I got way into that with the effects.

MATTHEWS And then he'd play a lot of Eastern-sounding scales and weird drums on the guitar.

When you first started playing together, were you doing Dave's songs?

MATTHEWS Not really, not for a while. We started recording stuff in my basement or over at his house. I remember Joseph, his son, playing the drums with the balls on the end of the sticks. We'd do some silly recordings. It was open because we hadn't yet been defined.

We had fun together, and then I, sort of at the [suggestion] of Tim and a few other people, started the Matthews Band. A couple of songs had been written before the band, but we worked them up and started playing them. And it was only really after that that Tim and I got together and started playing acoustically. Remember we did the Prism [coffeehouse] thing? That was the first time the two of us played two acoustics together.

Tim was also involved in the band's first album. Dave, what were you looking for him to bring into those sessions?

MATTHEWS Tim and I had been playing acoustic gigs, and it just made sense to bring Tim in, to have some of that spirit, the vibe we had together.

Tim, did you play more acoustic or electric on the early band albums?

REYNOLDS Actually a lot of acoustic. I'd spend about two months playing acoustic and three days playing electric.

MATTHEWS It was us sitting next to each other, strumming madly. It was so much fun.

REYNOLDS We sat in the studio just like this [*moves chair right in front of Matthews*] with a glass thing [between us], and that's how we did the whole first record. The band was all on the second floor.

MATTHEWS And then they'd inevitably turn his acoustic guitar way up and mine way down! That's [producer Steve] Lillywhite—I'm not saying whether he was right or wrong, but he'd say [*affects British accent*], "OK, let's turn David down and Timmy up" [*laughs*]. I love how with the last album, he said, "David, you don't really feature on this album at all, but don't tell anyone." We'd learn it, we'd all play, and then he'd turn me down.

Were you playing the same parts?

REYNOLDS On the first album we played the same part and then doubled it—like four acoustic guitars playing the same thing.

MATTHEWS And it made it sound really huge.

REYNOLDS I would just overdub a little bit. I did more electric overdubs as the albums went on.

MATTHEWS The last one [*Before These Crowded Streets*] has a lot more production. We still recorded the rhythm section live—guitar, bass, and drums—but then much more stuff went on top. Oh, put Stick there, piano . . . it doesn't matter if they're not in the band. We had a lot of other people. And Tim taped his face up and played lots of electric overdubs.

Dave, have you always played exclusively acoustic?

MATTHEWS I never really played electric. Sometimes when I pick one up, I'm surprised. It's amazing how suddenly you're just like [*makes wailing rock lead sounds*]. Yeah, I know what that feels like now! And then I put it down, and I just sit back down with an acoustic.

What drew you to playing an acoustic in the first place?

MATTHEWS I think in the first place it was a percussive thing. Also it's lighter and there are less things you need with it, so when I was younger and just traveling around, doing a lot of walking, it was always easier to have an acoustic. So I sort of grew attached to how portable it was. And when you're 16 and you can play "Father and Son" by Cat Stevens, [*sings*] "It's not time to make a change . . ." all of a sudden you're making out.

It's interesting that you've always played an acoustic, because you hardly ever play standard acoustic guitar open-position chords. Instead, you favor a lot of closed positions and up-the-neck things that are more typical of electric playing. How did that style evolve?

MATTHEWS I think one of the biggest inspirations was John D'earth. He's a trumpet player and a great teacher as well; he did the string arrangements on the last album. But he once said to me, "Guitarists always write everything in E or A or D." So I started playing as many things as I could that were a half step away.

Do you come up with those closed-position patterns by hunting and pecking?

MATTHEWS A lot of things that I do come out of trying to find circular motions. I'll just go around and around with something—unlike Tim. I think one reason we're complementary is that I can play the same five notes in the same order for an hour and find it absolutely satisfying. And Tim can swim around; I don't know if Tim ever repeats himself. So then the two of us kind of land comfortably together.

One of your signature guitar parts is the staccato "Satellite" riff, which opens up a lot of possibilities for Tim to play more sustained or legato types of things. It's not like playing over a big strum.

REYNOLDS Yeah, exactly. It's clearly different, especially where there are just two guitars. With a band you can come up with a really simple part, because everyone else is laying down a lot of other stuff. But with two acoustic guitars, you have to be more aware of [the other guitar part].

Tim, do you come up with the guitar melodies you play in "Satellite" and other songs when you're jamming?

Matthews with DMB fiddler Boyd Tinsley.

REYNOLDS I just come up with it in the studio, and Steve, the producer, says, "Stick with that." And that becomes the theme.

It becomes part of the song.

MATTHEWS It really does. And people get excited when they hear that. When the band is live and Tim is not with us, I don't think people generally miss things, but people definitely react [when they hear that guitar line]. With "Crash," when they hear the little signature things that Timmy does, the pull-offs and stuff, they go "Yaaaah!" It's almost more familiar than everything else.

REYNOLDS The [duo] thing is like a band. Because we play with bands, we hear a lot more in our heads than what we play. The psychic vibe of a band comes in, and we just lock in like a band.

MATTHEWS Sometimes I'm amazed by how it locks in, really amazed.

There are a lot of songs on the live record with intense drone parts. I'm thinking, for instance, of "Warehouse."

REYNOLDS Oh yeah, I tune this down [*tunes sixth string down to B*]. And then I have this pedal that in the backward mode can make it go up an octave or down. I set it so that it will go down. So I get this drone going and repeat it and then I make it go down an octave. You can't get too busy with the backward mode—it starts to pile up. But the chip lets it bleed off naturally, so we turn it off and just stop. You can do a lot of stuff where you play one thing and then it'll repeat a couple of times and you can actually play your next part, so there are two, three things going on at once just for a minute.

MATTHEWS That definitely gets into a nice wall. So by the time we get into the body of the song, when it sucks back, this little window opens.

Tim, do you ever feel limited when you're using effects with an acoustic guitar?

REYNOLDS No, it's the opposite. I play so much electric guitar that I get my ya-yas out with that, and when I'm playing acoustic, I don't ever feel I need that. I get off on doing both.

I can play acoustic guitar without effects—I practice that way, and I've made records without them—but I like to have more colors. I have lots of records of acoustic guitars, but I don't listen to them as much as I listen to other records that have a lot more sounds. But that's just my own taste, and my tastes always change, so that's only today.

"Minarets," "The Last Stop," and other songs make heavy use of Middle Eastern-sounding scales.

REYNOLDS Yeah. I used to like bebop because it had a zillion chords, but then I kind of overloaded on that concept and got into Eastern music, which is just one chord, and I could relate to John Lee Hooker again. And that opened up a whole different way of improvising, based on sound as opposed to notes, and then mixing them together again. You know, you can play just one note forever [*plays note with slow, watery bend*]. You're just messing around there instead of like [*plays fast bop-style lines*]—the nervous Western industrial society approach. Am I penis yet? [*Laughter.*] For hyper people like me, that's a great energy.

MATTHEWS But then Tim can access both of those.

REYNOLDS John McLaughlin is known for going ape shit, right? But with Shakti, he does these beautiful opening bits, the Indian approach. He does these beautiful bends, Ravi Shankar kind of stuff where he bends it so much you can hear him tune the guitar back up during the song.

Dave, what inspired you to explore Eastern territory in your songwriting?

MATTHEWS I get inspired by Tim a lot, but it's also a place that I haven't gone to and have always loved. If you're playing something like [*plays rhythmic drone on two strings*], eventually, if you don't like it, you're not listening [*laughs*]. And then after a while, when you go [*drops drone down one step*] or just a tiny change, it makes it so dramatic.

REYNOLDS With Steve Lillywhite, any time you do any Eastern thing, he goes, "Oh, it's Adrian Belew." Because that's his only reference point for anything like that. You're doing a deep raga and he goes, "Oh, it's Adrian Belew." It's like, Steve, take your rich ass over to India for awhile [*laughter*].

Dave's songs start with his guitar but take on a different identity when the band arranges them. Is it hard to go back and play them with two guitars and forget about what all the other instruments were doing?

MATTHEWS It's easy to forget about everything else that was going on. Some songs are a bit of a challenge—there are certain songs that we haven't even tried. "Crush" was one that I didn't know if it would work out. For some reason, in the studio [with the band] that song was a

DAVE MATTHEWS' RHYTHM STYLE

Like Richard Thompson, Ani DiFranco, and other top songwriter-guitarists, Dave Matthews has developed a potent and highly individual guitar style that is inextricably linked to his songwriting. He sticks to standard tuning, with an occasional sixth-string drop to D, but uses a chord vocabulary that is anything but standard. During the course of our interview, Matthews demonstrated the rhythm parts from numerous songs, and some clear stylistic patterns emerged.

First, Matthews is far less bound by open strings than most acoustic players, which is one reason why he never uses a capo. He's as comfortable playing in a key like G♯ ("Satellite"), without using even a single open string, as in the usual E, G, A, and D. The same goes for his drone-oriented parts. While "Minarets," for example, is in the open-string-friendly key of E (played up in seventh position to get octave E's on the fifth and sixth strings), he plays an equally driving drone in "Warehouse" in the key of B (also up in seventh position) with no open strings. Even when he tunes to dropped D, it isn't necessarily for playing in the key of D; in "Crush," he tunes down but plays in Bm and never hits the sixth string open in the entire song. So why retune? To facilitate off-the-beaten-track fingerings.

Matthews' preference for closed chords means, of course, using plenty of barre chords, often reduced to two- and three-note modal voicings (without the third, neither major nor minor). Watching him navigate through numerous progressions, I was struck by how economical his parts are; typically, he goes to one position and stays put, making whatever stretches are necessary to reach the notes rather than moving around the neck. "Satellite" is a case in point: the main riff is a little circle of notes played on the bottom three strings while his index finger stays planted at the fourth fret. (Tim Reynolds, by contrast, plays the same riff by moving down the neck.)

By steering away from garden-variety open chords and keys, Matthews sets his songs apart from most guitar-based music right from the downbeat. There are other advantages to this style: Closed positions allow more control over string percussion, which he uses heavily, particularly in the duo with Reynolds. And when Matthews does opt for an open chord, it makes a dramatic contrast—an instant lift for a chorus or a bridge.

struggle. Finally we just said, "Well, let's just play it real straight." Then Fonzi [bassist Stefan Lessard] found this groove that was like Marvin Gaye, and we were like, "Oh, that's good." And so the song fell in there when the Marvin Gaye came out, at least in the bass.

I just never thought of this song after that as being something that would work without that feel, and it was a really pleasant surprise when Tim and I played it. It was just [*snaps fingers*]. It's really natural. It doesn't sound forced.

When you're playing with just two guitars, do you find that you play more percussively?

MATTHEWS Yeah. It doesn't come out as much with a band, you know. If I were using one of these [full-body acoustic] guitars, I don't know if it would work. I use a Chet Atkins because it's like [*makes sharp sound*].

REYNOLDS It's hard for an acoustic to cut through with all the instruments.

MATTHEWS Exactly. That's why it's so amazing when rock bands use acoustic guitars where it's like [*strums open A-minor chord; stops and makes wretching sound*]. Stop that, please, Bob!

A lot of times a part like that becomes just a little texture, especially if you throw an electric guitar on top of it. In your band arrangements, you manage to avoid that trap, even though there's a lot going on. Your guitar has its place.

MATTHEWS Yes. But I guess it's also the fact that there isn't an electric guitar all the time. It's not based around that. When we're doing albums or when Tim is playing with the band, it adds, but not everything is built around screaming rock guitar. There's a little more space.

How much arranging do you do for playing as a duo?

REYNOLDS We know these songs almost in the way that someone who's played standards for years plays those songs every night, and can go anywhere with them. In a second you can tell this is the bridge. . . . It's almost like the music plays us, we play it so much. And when you play them that much, you don't give them life if you play them by rote; they have to change every night.

DISCOGRAPHY

**DAVE MATTHEWS
AND TIM REYNOLDS**
Live at Luther College, Bama
Rags/RCA 67755 (1999).

TIM REYNOLDS
See into Your Soul, TR Music (2000).
Solo acoustic guitar. Available through
www.timreynolds.com or Bama
Rags (see page 123).
Stream, TR Music (2000).
Reissue of 1993 acoustic album.
Tim Reynolds Live: Puke Matrix Tour,
TR Music (1999). Electric trio set.
Gossip of the Neurons, TR Music
(1996). Solo acoustic-electric
guitar improv, recorded
live at Millers.

MATTHEWS I'm impressed when I see bands that just come out and do a note-for-note thing of their album, which is really like classical music. I'm impressed by that, because it must be *hard.* I would go out of my tree.

REYNOLDS When I was in Secrets, it was a great fusion band and there was improvising, but 99 percent of the time was all this synchronized tight shit. And that can get really boring fast, 'cause I like to improvise. I realized then that I wasn't cut out to be a fusion guy or anything like that. I had to be much looser.

[Dave's] songs give you an emotional thing, to open different chakras. It's real music, like all the ragas have a different meaning and emotion, and his songs cover all those colors.

How would you compare the whole experience of performing with the band versus the duo?

MATTHEWS I love playing with the band. I really, really love it. But there are more personalities; obviously there's still the joy, there's still the generosity, but it's more like there's a choreography about it. You have to be more aware of each other, and there's sometimes the threat of falling a little too much into habit.

With Tim, though, it's so intimate, it's like going out for a candlelit dinner, except we're not eating. And I also feel that to a certain degree, if I was to suddenly go [*makes jibberish noises*], in this environment, Tim would probably laugh. I don't know if it would be an appropriate thing to do with the band. There's a certain looseness about when the two of us are playing that's really beautiful and really different from the band. I feel like this is real precious, you know. The band, I'm amazed how quiet we can get, but Tim and I can get [*whispers*] real quiet.

How about from your side, Tim?

REYNOLDS Different layers of it are different. In the upper layers, you're playing a different instrument, different size crowds. Acoustic has more subtle things because there's no rhythm section, so you're not competing with more sound. Yet when you have a rhythm section, that allows you a different kind of melodic freedom.

So it's different but it's the same, because the more you get down to the ground layer of where it comes from, *we're* being played. Music is playing us, and we let it go the way it should go. Even if it's just for a second, that second lasts a long time. Whatever creates that is really the ultimate.

Unlike a lot of people who perform with rock bands, who get sort of timid when they unplug, all the intensity and dynamics are there in your acoustic show.

MATTHEWS I know what you mean, when you go out and watch a band unplugged—especially if they try to bust out some mean electric licks. And it's like, "Don't do any of these, unless it's in humor—the acoustic will not be an electric guitar for you."

DISCOGRAPHY

DAVE MATTHEWS BAND
Listener Supported, Bama Rags/RCA 67898 (1999).
Before These Crowded Streets, RCA 67660 (1998).
Live at Red Rocks 8.15.95, Bama Rags/RCA 67587 (1997).
Crash, RCA 66904 (1996).
Under the Table and Dreaming, RCA 66449 (1994).
Recently (five-song EP), Bama Rags 2 (1994).
Remember Two Things, Bama Rags 1 (1993). Bama Rags, LLC, PO Box 1911, Charlottesville, VA 22903; (804) 971-4829; www.dmband.com.

REYNOLDS And then someone like John Hammond can *rock* on an acoustic. It's amazing.

Some of the covers that you do are surprising, like John Prine's "Angel from Montgomery."

MATTHEWS I'd love to do Bonnie Raitt's version of that. We did a Marilyn Manson song last year ["Cryptorchid"]. We turned it into a beautiful song. It was great to play this lovely, sorrow-filled ballad about the arrival of bitterness and sadness and suicidal tendencies; I'd sing it, and then afterward say, "That's a tune by Marilyn Manson" [*laughs*].

In your set, it's interesting to hear a song like "Angel from Montgomery," which has a standard folk/country chord progression, next to your songs, which almost never have standard progressions.

MATTHEWS But I love it in other people's tunes. I don't know why I can't write like that. I love tunes like "Wild Horses" or [Lyle Lovett's] "Boat"—what a great song. I can't do it like him—he's got such a great delivery.

WHAT THEY PLAY (1999)

The Dave Matthews and Tim Reynolds acoustic tour crew arrives with a truckload of road cases, but it's almost entirely PA and recording gear; the actual stuff used on stage would fit easily into the back of a Honda. At sound check, Matthews' longtime friend and guitar tech Monk Montgomery even apologizes about the simplicity of the stage setup as he walks me through it.

Reynolds plays two Martin D-35s: a '96 and a '93. Both have Martin's standard Fishman pickups, which run into a Morley volume pedal, a Boss digital delay, and then a Countryman direct box. The little Boss stomp box is the source of all of Reynolds' electronic trickery. "There's one backwards mode—it plays infinite, and you can mess with that," Reynolds says. "And there are delay modes that you can go infinite. There are a lot of cool little things."

For these duo shows, Matthews' main ax is a Martin HD-28, also Fishman equipped (the Gold Plus Natural 2) and running straight into a Countryman DI. "Even on the big tours we use Fishman," Montgomery says, "because it's really bright, and the way he plays so hard and a lot of low notes, it's the only thing that really captures the sound." Both Matthews' and Reynolds' guitars are miked (with a B&K 4051-A and an Audio-Technica 4021, respectively), but the signal only goes onto the night's board tape, not to the house. The Matthews crew (as well as fans) are inveterate tapers, and their archives are the source of releases like *Live at Luther College* and the DMB's *Live at Red Rocks*.

Matthews' backup six-string is a Lakewood M-32, which has its own integrated pickup system. And for a handful of songs—"Wild Horses," "Spoon," and "The Last Stop"—he picks up a Martin D-12-28 12-string. (For "The Last Stop," it's tuned down a half step.)

All these guitars are strung with D'Addario lights. No funky tunings, and no capos or other gizmos except for Reynolds' slide. "Sorry, that's it," Montgomery says with a shrug. "I sit in that chair all night."

For band tours, Matthews has long been playing a Gibson Chet Atkins model that has been modified with Fishman electronics and runs through API preamps, Meyer CP-10 EQs, and Eventide harmonizers. The Chet's thin, feedback-free sound, Matthews says, helps to cut through the dense band mix.

When I listen to your songs for the first time, the parts almost always go somewhere other than where I think they're going to go.

MATTHEWS Maybe a lot of that comes from a blatant lack of knowledge. In some ways, I'm freed up by the fact that I don't write—

REYNOLDS —that you haven't had chord progressions shoved down your throat, so you have a different way of looking at them. That's the shit, though, that's what makes it different. That's why most people, after they've learned everything, spend [so much time] unlearning. That's why when I used to play jazz, and I would write songs, I would never write a jazz song, because it would sound like jazz. I always liked it when it was something like an accident. Like John Lee Hooker talks about, "I never do my changes on the four or the eight, because that's what people expect of me. I don't even know what I'm going to do—I just do it the way I like it."

I think of the typical verse/chorus/bridge structure of a song as a little wheel that keeps turning at a predictable speed. Your songs are more expansive than that; their structure is less obvious.

MATTHEWS With some songs, I think about the sections forward and backward—like maybe here's the main body of the song, and then there's a sort of chorus, and then the main body of the song, then I'll do the sort of chorus again, but maybe I'll do it twice as long, then I'll have another chorus, then the next one I'll do twice as long. I think of a lot of it in math—not clearly in math, but like, "Well, that makes sense. That's balanced."

REYNOLDS Music is math without the formulas—

MATTHEWS —without the problem of ascribing.
   And then I write a lot in patterns. Like "Satellite" I started off as this [*plays dissonant fingering exercise*]. And we sometimes do that [in concert]—that's fun. It's amazing, people recognize it. And then when they're convinced it's the wrong song, we play it the right way.

That song sounds a lot more sinister that way. It's like the satellite that they've lost track of over at mission control.

MATTHEWS The one that's fucking up all the telephones! That's the one I'm voting for.

BEN HARPER

With alternative rock and a roots-music revival in full swing in the '90s,

perhaps it was inevitable that a musician would come along and bridge

those two worlds. That person was Ben Harper, whose childhood in the

thick of the southern California folk scene (his family has run the

Claremont Folk Music Center for two generations) gave him an

effortless kind of fluency in the traditions and techniques of American

roots music, as well as exposure to masters such as Taj Mahal and

David Lindley, who took him under their wings.

Scores of young guitar players have been inspired by Harper's

irresistible grooves and in-the-pocket slide work—in fact, he has helped

to bring the acoustic lap slide guitar out of near extinction. At the time

of this 1999 interview, Harper had just surprised fans with the largely

electric CD *Burn to Shine,* and he was spreading the gospel on big

stages across the U.S. and Europe, where he (like many other American

roots-oriented musicians) enjoys widespread popularity. The summer of

2000 found Harper hooked up with yet another high-profile rock tour—

this time with the hard-jamming Dave Matthews Band.

NEXT GENERATION BLUES

Ben Harper has traveled one incredibly unlikely path to where he sits tonight, testifying in front of a packed amphitheater on a wild array of lap steel, acoustic, and electric guitars. He arrived on the scene in the early '90s as a folk blues prodigy, coaxing gorgeous tones from an obscure vintage specimen, the Weissenborn lap slide guitar, and spiking his repertoire with acoustic reggae and roots rock. Fast-forward a few years, and he had forged a connection with the alt-rock world—touring with Pearl Jam and P.J. Harvey—and had begun experimenting with feedback and distortion on his Weissenborns, creating a spectacularly heavy rock sound that would segue right back into hushed acoustic balladry. Fast-forward again to 1999, when in the wake of headlining the HORDE festival with his band, the Innocent Criminals, Harper added the solid-body electric to his guitar arsenal for the first time on his album *Burn to Shine*, mixing folk-influenced tunes with Led Zeppelin–esque rock, soulful R&B, churning Rolling Stones boogie, even a dash of old-time New Orleans jazz.

All of these sides of Harper's musical personality are on display on this balmy fall evening at Berkeley, California's Greek Theater, where Harper demonstrates why he's become the roots-music ambassador of his generation. It's a role he seems to have been born for, as he reveals in a backstage conversation while the Funky Meters sound-check upstairs.

So is this kind of a strange time to be talking with Acoustic Guitar *magazine, given all the voltage running through* Burn to Shine?

HARPER It's the perfect time. It will give me the opportunity to explain a couple of critical things about myself and about music. I don't feel that I need to qualify this album in talking to *Acoustic Guitar*, but I do feel the need just to make the statement that I plan on making music for a long, long time. The foundation of the music that I make is extremely acoustic-based—folk, blues, Delta blues—and the songs I write are on acoustic slide guitar and acoustic guitar.

But I do have to say that playing and expressing myself on electrics of late is renewing my focus and enthusiasm and excitement about acoustics. If I played only acoustic for my entire life, I would get bored. So for my own musical growth, I need to venture out into other worlds of music and sound. [*Burn to Shine*] is not an abandonment—not by a long shot, because there are songs like "Two Hands of a Prayer" and "In the Lord's Arms" . . .

In the past you've said that when you'd pick up a solid-body electric, it wouldn't feel like you somehow. What has changed along the way?

HARPER There was a time when I couldn't see myself playing electric, but I've been extremely influenced by a youth rock community. When I started doing shows, even with *Welcome to the Cruel World,* which was all acoustic, there were no singer-songwriters at my gigs. Pearl Jam came down to my gigs, P.J. Harvey. . . . I was more embraced by a rock community in the beginning, and that had an influence on me musically. These people were coming to my shows, and I started getting hip to their music. It was just a natural progression.

I would think that the kinds of large venues you wound up playing would have had an effect too.

HARPER Yeah, that's been exciting—to be able to bring acoustic-based music to large audiences that aren't necessarily there to see you. I'll never forget opening up for P.J. Harvey—she invited us to tour with her. I'd sit down with an acoustic Weissenborn in front of 12-year-old girls with black eyeliner packed in the front row, looking up at me going, "What in the hell is he playing?" But by the third or fourth song, the heads would start to nod, and then it would be on, you know. We never got stoned or anything like that—not yet.

When I first heard you perform back in '94, I was struck by the fact that the music on record sounded very intimate, but when you got on stage you really expanded it for the setting.

HARPER Every time we've made a record, by the time we've taken it to the stage, we're leaps and bounds beyond our ability at the time we made the record. But we only got to those heightened abilities by making the record. So by the time we've toured for three months, the song is new again.

What are some of the new abilities you've found recently?

HARPER I don't know . . . a comfort and a confidence. I've said oftentimes that playing live is the most intensified form of practice, and it will push you to grow faster than any amount of hours of rehearsal. I feel that from a guitar-playing perspective, I've just put in a lot of time playing slide and round-neck, and that is reflected on this record. I feel a kinship with the craft and the spirit of songwriting compared with feeling more like a distant relative in the past. And singing as well— I feel like this was the first record that I really found my voice.

Would you say that performing also has a lot to do with the growth in your singing?

HARPER Yeah, it's pushed me and my abilities. Through performing hundreds of nights a year, your voice is either going to give out or get stronger. And the reason it hasn't given out is that I don't allow the addictive side of my personality to control my life—drinking and smoking and carrying on like that. I don't find any romance in any of that. I'd rather have water and be done with it.

One of the biggest surprises on Burn to Shine *is the title track, with that classic electric rock 'n' roll guitar groove. What inspired you to plug in to that sound?*

HARPER I've been writing songs in that style for a while, and I chose to bring out songs that would give the album a new musical direction and dimension. I could have done all of these songs acoustic, but I wanted to bring in new sounds that have been inspiring me over the past couple years.

You have to somehow branch out into other styles to improve your own style—within reason; I don't see myself making a drum-and-bass record or a techno record. I like the music, but I don't see it as me.

Speaking of branching out, how about that song "Susie Blue," with the Dixieland tenor banjo and horns. Did you write that song on guitar?

HARPER I wrote that on guitar, and when it came out, the chords fit that style of music. It so happened that in the town I grew up in, which is Claremont, in the Inland Empire, east of L.A. about an hour, there's a really good coffeehouse called Nick's Café. That's one of the coffeehouses where I did my first gigs. There's a Dixieland-style jazz band that played for the last 15 years every Thursday night. And I thought to myself, man, how good would that be? The chords to "Susie Blue" just fit their style, and they agreed to do it. But I didn't play guitar on that track.

It's nice to hear you play with David Lindley on Burn to Shine. *I know your connection goes way back—I remember hearing his cover of your song "Mama's Got a Girlfriend Now" long before I heard you. When was your first encounter with him?*

HARPER It would be impossible [to say]. My parents and him and his wife were friends before I was born—it goes back that far. Growing up, I was privileged—his daughter and I are friends, and we grew up together very, very close, like a brother and sister, really. We used to travel around with him, go to shows and see him play and stuff like that. I would intensely, unconsciously, and not knowing why, focus on his playing at a very young age.

My parents have a music store in the Inland Empire called the Folk Music Center, and he used to come in all the time. We'd hang out and have laughs—he's just the funniest guy.

How did he wind up playing on "In the Lord's Arms"?

HARPER I knew he had stopped doing session work, and I was like, damn, the only person that can really bring this song to life in the way that I hear it is David Lindley. I mean, I did have some David Lindley clout, if you want to call it that, so I figured OK, I'll give it a shot. I was nervous as hell and I left the message on his machine. A day or two went by and I got a call, "Hey, man. It's Lindley. I'd love to do it." I couldn't believe it—I was floored.

When he came into the studio, he brought the most incredible selection of instruments—the most amazing Gibson mandolin, the most amazing fiddle—tuned every one of them by ear to A440, perfect pitch, like nothing I've ever seen, and we laid it down. And it was one of the best musical experiences of my life to date.

Aside from the lap slide connection, you both have deep folk roots combined with a love of percussion and reggae-inspired grooves.

HARPER He's a huge influence, there's no question. David Lindley and guys like Taj Mahal—huge influences on me, immeasurable. And the fact that these guys are still alive makes life much more exciting and livable for me. David knows Pete Seeger, he knows Bess Hawes, he knows Jean Ritchie, the dulcimer player. David knew Okie Adams, an old-school banjo maker. Flatt and Scruggs. He knew all those guys. Taj knew Mississippi John Hurt, Fred McDowell, Lonnie Johnson, Brownie McGhee. . . . So for me, they're a direct link to that school.

Did you come into contact with those people in the music store in your childhood?

HARPER My mom is an incredible singer and acoustic guitar player, and I've been going to see Taj Mahal since the time I was six years old—we used to go when there'd be all-ages shows at the Santa Barbara Bowl and stuff like that. And David as well—being exposed to his music at a young age has played a large role in the music that I make. David used to play with this amazing percussionist, [Ras] Baboo, who had a profound effect on me. I really wonder what happened to him. He was the first percussionist in El Rayo X, and he just brought the show to life in an amazing way.

What does your experience working in the store and repairing instruments as a teenager mean for you now as a player? Do you still do any tinkering?

HARPER Man, I miss guitar repair and construction. I had just touched on construction when I left my parents' shop, but I had worked in restoration. There's a luthier in Glendale who worked for Gibson in the '40s named Jack Willock, who I apprenticed with for guitar repair and restoration for five years. Jack Willock is a magic man—he knew Lloyd Loar and worked in the factory before he went off to war, and what he taught me about life and guitar repair is more important than I could ever say.

I do still get inside of certain instruments from time to time, and anytime I get off, I work in my parents' shop and help run the store. I set up the instruments on the wall, making sure that when customers come in the action is set well and playable, and things like that. But I've taken too much time away from [repair]. If I would have stuck with that, by now I'd be pretty good, but I just don't have enough time lately. I've got a guy who does all my work, Billy Asher in Santa Monica, who's just got incredible hands, and I trust him like I trust myself.

Generally speaking, how would you compare instruments from the '20s and '30s with new instruments and new reproductions of vintage instruments?

HARPER I like new instruments that sound so good you don't care whether they're new or not. Like the Matons. That's really what I look for. The old instruments, it's kind of an unfair advantage, because imagine an instrument that was made in 1920 or 1930—the tree that produced the wood dates back into the 1800s. In a certain way, it's unfair to put the new up against the old. And in another way, that's the standard by which all good guitars should be measured.

But I'm not one of those vintage snobs; if the guitar is nice and sounds good and has songs waiting for me in it, I'm ready to get on it. Like the Martin—that vintage reissue herringbone 000-28, Indian rosewood, beautiful piece of spruce on the top. It's a new Martin, but I don't care. It's got the stuff.

Let's talk about your playing style. Many of your earlier songs played on a regular acoustic guitar, like "Ashes" or the 12-string piece "Number 3," sound as if they're in a low version of standard tuning—down a step or more.

HARPER Yeah, D to D instead of E to E, some of them.

Is that something that you did to match your voice better or because of the sound?

HARPER It was the sound. I loved the way the guitar resonated in D to D at the time; it just felt right in my hands and my voice. I'm back up to E now, doing a lot of stuff in 440, like "In the Lord's Arms" and "Two Hands of a Prayer."

And you also play with your thumb rather than a pick, right? That muted sound you get seems like such a natural match for the way you sing— it's like the instrumental version of your voice.

HARPER I totally agree with that statement. Yeah, it's a thumb and finger sort of brush. I stole that from my mom.

Do you use regular light strings when you tune down?

HARPER Light or medium—you can go medium without worrying about the neck when you tune down, in most cases. But even lights will do it, give you sort of a bendability that's really fun to play with. It's interesting, I think A440 was established with gut strings, at a time when there were no steel strings, and it does feel natural to have the steel-string guitar down that low. I kind of go by the guitar [deciding] where to tune it, even forgetting about my voice, because I can pretty much handle the step up for my voice. Guitars sort of have a natural place they want to be; even if it's a half step down, I'll go there.

It gets tricky, because I'm very particular in my tone from the acoustic guitar, and different acoustics have different qualities. People want to know, "What brand acoustic do you play?" It's like, hey, it's not that easy. The best-sounding acoustic guitar might not translate to be the best one on stage—it might be this full, rich, balanced tone, but when you get it on stage, it just is too boomy and there are too many other things going on. So I've got different guitars for different purposes.

On the lap guitars, do you tend to make up tunings for particular songs, or are there a few tunings that you generally use?

HARPER I make up tunings per song, but I do have a sort of regimented tuning that I use quite a bit. It's D A D D A D—dad dad, call it. You can also go to C G C C G C or B F♯ B B F♯ B, and I've even gone to

A E A A E A. "God Fearing Man" is tuned all the way down to low A with heavy strings on an acoustic Weissenborn run through a Marshall or something.

Having just the root and fifth in the tuning makes a lot of sense, because a lot of what you're playing are two-note power chords.

HARPER Oh, they're straight from the power-chord school. It gives me a working chord all the way up the neck, without that higher third string [as in regular open-D tuning, D A D F♯ A D] that can throw certain chords off. And I use [open-D] tuning as well, like on "Pleasure and Pain."

You also intersperse some 12-string here and there. The song "Jah Work" has some fantastic 12-string lead on it.

HARPER I've got to confess, that's Al Anderson from Bob Marley and the Wailers. What he did on 12-string on that was stunning.

But 12-string, I love it. I love Leo Kottke—he's been a big influence with his fingerpicking and melodies and things. I don't know how the guy does it, man. I mean, Leo Kottke must have hands of steel.

When you arrange new songs with your band, do you find yourself changing the original guitar parts in light of what the other instruments are doing?

HARPER I may change a guitar part a little bit or do something to improve it, but I rarely abandon it, because that's usually the biggest part of the song. There's definitely an aspect of adapting to the moment, but usually it's the other way around—nine times out of ten, the other instruments construct themselves around what the guitar is doing.

Do you work on writing lyrics as a separate process from coming up with the guitar parts and melodies?

HARPER There are three different musical worlds that go on in my life at once. There's the dimension of crafting the melodies and lyrics. I've got a hundred pieces of paper—scraps, hotel stationery—and then a constant work-in-progress Walkman tape. Then there's the other side of me that just writes songs in one sitting at one time—it's the straight, lightning-bolt channel. And then right in the center there's this stream of consciousness, and I'll sit down and rattle off whatever comes to mind and write five pages of garbage. For my songwriting, that's the trinity.

Which of your songs have come from the lightning-bolt channel?

HARPER "Widow of a Living Man" came with no explanation and no warning. It was like, oh, I'd better sit down and do this. And boom, the song is done.

"Two Hands of a Prayer," from Burn to Shine, *is a complex piece. Was that the product of a lot of crafting?*

HARPER Yeah, that was crafted. I had two pages of ideas for that song, and I was going to take it from where it was into this sort of rock affair, a "Stairway to Heaven" type of vibe. It was already close to eight minutes long and I had this whole other movement for it, but it wasn't taking me anywhere, so I kept it where it was.

Burn to Shine *has a nice balance of dark, heavy-sounding tunes with breezy, fun stuff like "Susie Blue" and "Steal My Kisses." Do you get that kind of balance by cutting back from a big pool of songs?*

HARPER It's been different ways. For *Welcome to the Cruel World,* we had just the right amount of songs—not one more, not one less, it was just the album. And then for *Fight for Your Mind,* we had like 20 songs that we had planned to record—*Fight for Your Mind* almost was a double album, but costs started getting up there and we wanted to get the album out by a certain time, and it was just down to the wire. So we had to not only drop a couple off, we had to not record some and stop recording a couple others. With *Will to Live,* it was a similar situation. So with [*Burn to Shine*], we just picked the songs we knew were going to be on the record, 'cause those alone took more time than we had expected.

DISCOGRAPHY

CD Box Collection (includes
   Harper's first three albums),
   Virgin 46694 (2000).
Burn to Shine, Virgin 48151 (1999).
The Will to Live, Virgin 44178 (1997).
Fight for Your Mind, Virgin 40620 (1995).
Welcome to the Cruel World,
   Virgin 39320 (1994).

Thinking back, one of the things that was so striking about your first album, which was so unusual for a young player, was your focus on things like tone and groove as opposed to flexing chops and playing riffs. Were there any particular players who modeled that quality for you?

HARPER For me, it would be hard to explain that, because that's just who I am musically.I come from a place that is groove oriented. I have a deep love for hip-hop music and blues, soul, rock. I love what Zeppelin did with electric and acoustic, and Hendrix as well.

As somebody who grew up around so much country blues, what's your perspective on the '90s phenomenon of Robert Johnson becoming something of a pop star?

HARPER I know, the guy has sold like a million records, hasn't he? Man, I think it's the best thing ever. I remember when I was in junior high school and high school, trying to bring up Robert Johnson to some of my friends, and they would just laugh. They're like, "What on earth is this?"

It's odd because to me, Mississippi John Hurt has always been a pop star. There was never any line between John Hurt and the Bee Gees, besides the fact that the Bee Gees were on the radio. The Bee Gees, John Hurt, and the Clash—it was all just music to me. So it felt like, well of course Willie Dixon wrote "Little Red Rooster," which was the first hit by Led Zeppelin. Oh yeah, sure, the Rolling Stones—that's Fred McDowell. It was never any mystery.

But I think it's great; I think it's wicked. Now, I mean, you can walk into a Virgin megastore and there's just walls of Washboard Sam and Skip James, just walls of it. That's really exciting.

Do you think that musicians are getting better informed about the roots of the music that they're playing?

HARPER I hope so. I can only speak through my perspective. If I didn't have all this music at my disposal for inspiration, I wouldn't be the player that I am, and I think it's crucial that groups and bands are able to grasp the importance of a Tim Hardin or a Skip James. To me, it's super important to understand the roots of music. I can never stress that enough—the importance of listening to and researching different musics.

I understand you have a new baby at home, as well as an older child. How has parenthood changed your musical life?

HARPER It's new life, so it's going to bring new life to what you do. That's what it's been for me. "Steal My Kisses" was inspired by my son. When he was about a year old, every time I'd reach in to give him a kiss, he always pushed me, like "Come on, Dad!" I think my beard scratched him. I'd always have to say, "All right, I'm going to steal one!" And he'd go, "No! No!" And then he'd put his hands down and I'd steal one real quick.

You know, it's just endless. [Kids] don't take any time away from the creative process—I just don't do other things. Nothing could take me away from music, because music is the majority of my consciousness. I live my life through song to a large degree. I have to write music in order

WHAT THEY PLAY (1999)

Ben Harper is a serious guitar fiend—so much so that every one of his albums includes a credit for collector/writer Ben Elder as "official researcher and advisor on Weissenborn and related instruments."

In the lap department, Harper has a major collection of '20s and '30s hollow-neck Weissenborns. The instrument heard all over *Welcome to the Cruel World* and *Fight for Your Mind* is a koa style 4. But ultimately, his Hendrix-goes-Hawaiian experiments with feedback and distortion (using an Ibanez TS-808 Tube Screamer run through a Demeter amp and a 4x10 Marshall) led him to search for alternatives to the old guitars, especially for stage use.

"In the studio, you can bring up the volume, but live, you don't have that luxury," he says. "You need the immediate volume to get on top of your band. And way before I would get to 12 o'clock, the [Weissenborns] were just blowing up, basically. They were getting an uncontrollable, unusable feedback that was so loud. It was like a bucking bronco. They were made with hide glue, and the sheer volume was rattling the ribs loose. Plus I slap them around a little bit—that doesn't help."

Harper's solution was to commission a new instrument from Santa Monica luthier Bill Asher. A cross between a Weissenborn and a solid-body electric, Asher's guitar is built with solid Honduras mahogany that is cut with eight hollow chambers and capped with koa. The Ben Harper model, now in limited production, has custom double-coil pickups wound by Tom Anderson. Harper's collection of Ashers includes several other pickup variations—one with two Seymour Duncan humbuckers, one with a Sunrise, and one with a humbucker and a Fernandes Sustainer.

Harper also plays a custom hollow-body lap steel made by the Australian company Maton Guitars that is equipped with a saddle pickup and an old Rickenbacker pickup—saddle for a clean acoustic-electric sound, the Rick for crunch (on the song "Forgiven," he switches back and forth on verse and chorus). For pure fuzz, he's been playing a Rickenbacker Electro. His slide of choice is made by Tim Scheerhorn.

As for round-neck guitars, Harper's vintage favorites are a 1958 Martin 00-18 (used heavily on his first two albums), a '40s Gibson LG-2, a '50s Gibson J-160, and a Guild 12-string (the last two are heard on *Burn to Shine*). His current stage acoustic is a custom Maton ECW80, a maple-bodied herringbone dreadnought with a built-in AP5 pickup/preamp system that Harper says is "phenomenal." All these instruments are strung with D'Addario phosphor-bronze lights.

The electrics heard on *Burn to Shine* include a '50s Gibson Melody Maker, a '57 Fender sunburst Strat, and a '50s Gibson Les Paul Junior. Harper's current stage show also includes a cameo by a Gibson EDS-1275 double-neck—originally a six/12 setup but now adapted with one six-string neck for slide and the other for standard playing.

to feel like I'm taking full advantage of breathing, and my wife understands that. But when you have kids, you just have to become superhuman. You have to be able to do what you do and be superdad.

How does it change your experience of the road?

HARPER Oh, it makes it painful. It makes it really hard to be away. And sooner than later, I'm going to have to step away from [being on] the road as much as I am right now.

How does the atmosphere of music in your house compare with what you grew up with? Is there a lot of music happening?

HARPER My son's favorites are Etta James and the Black Crowes—and Daddy. You know what I mean, he's down with Pops. And it's not like he's down because it's me. He just likes the music because he likes the sound of stuff.

There's music all the time. My wife loves music, and we're always playing. He's got his hands on all my instruments, and I've got a little drum set for him—he's always on it, and he's just loving it. And he loves to sing. So it's cool. I'm hoping I can plant that seed for him. It's not like I'm going to sign him up for guitar lessons by the time he's three or anything, but I just want to have that there for him.

I find that experiencing music with a child gives a whole new appreciation of the power of simple melodies. But that seems like a sense you've always had about music.

HARPER Yes. I refuse to let the music get in the way of the words or the words get in the way of the music by being too clever or too tricky, too cluttered. You have to leave room for both and have one reflect the other in a musical way. *Simplicity* is a tricky word, because it's not so simple to [achieve]. But I think it's just who I am—I communicate it straight ahead.

Clockwise from top left: Tyler Stewart, Jim Creeggan, Steven Page, Kevin Hearn, Ed Robertson.

BARENAKED LADIES

The band Barenaked Ladies, led by guitarists/songwriters Ed Robertson and Steven Page, makes a delicious contrast with many of the artists in this book, as they do in the rock scene as a whole. They were entertainers and natural-born comedians before becoming songwriters; rather than separate themselves from pop music in all its disposable varieties, they embrace it, and instead of self-consciously creating a larger-than-life image of themselves for the stage or the media, they present (and mock) themselves as regular guys. All of these qualities conspire to make them a blast of fresh air in the contemporary scene, and my two meetings with Robertson and Page—on the phone in 1998 and then in person in 2000—revealed what a pitch-perfect match these musicians are for each other.

The following conversation occurred at the beginning of a long arena tour, during a time when *Maroon* was just beginning to make its mark on rock radio and in the minds of BNL's young, clean-cut audience, many of whom have been following the band for years and sing along with every word of old favorites like "The Old Apartment" and "Brian Wilson," as well as continue the tradition of hurling macaroni at the mention of Kraft dinners in "If I Had $1,000,000."

THE BARENAKED ESSENTIALS

They just can't help themselves. During sound check at the Van Andel Arena in Grand Rapids, Michigan, there are only about 30 people sitting in the front row of the 12,000-seat venue, but the five guys called Barenaked Ladies are *already* putting on a little show, goofing around and chatting with the audience in between bits of rehearsal. Ed Robertson pauses from testing his rack of guitars to point out to this happy group of radio-station winners that a table of drinks and snacks is set out for them, and he and fellow front man Steven Page can't resist turning that announcement into an improvised ditty about "chips and pop." Later on, after smoothing out a few rough edges in songs from their brand-new album, *Maroon,* the band starts surfing through the pop catalog from "Tears of a Clown" to some English Beat to the opening verse of "Lucy in the Sky with Diamonds" with the phrase "marmalade skies" replaced by "pistol-whipped guys." The huge, garish jester's mask that looms over them (and whose open mouth and lapping tongue is their stage entrance) is the perfect backdrop: this is a band with entertaining in its blood and a highly developed taste for the absurd.

Even though the band's gift for high-wire improv and hilarity has been central to its rise from a Canadian cult success to one of modern rock's biggest acts, what is so unique about Barenaked Ladies is how seriously they take the business of not taking themselves too seriously.

Robertson and Page are two of the sharpest and wittiest craftsmen in pop songwriting today, often sneaking dark emotions into songs that have audiences boogying and belting out the chorus. They have also successfully whittled the overblown corporate-rock sound down to the essentials, remaining doggedly acoustic for most of the band's life until their 1998 blockbuster album *Stunt* introduced a taut mix of acoustic and electric elements, an instrumental expansion that continues on *Maroon.*

After pressing the flesh with their sound check audience, Page and Robertson join me backstage for a chat about songwriting and the 12-year rise of their band. Not only are they riding the release of *Maroon,* their deepest and best set of songs to date, but a highly entertaining movie called *Barenaked in America* (directed by avid BNL fan Jason Priestley), which follows the band on tour after the release of *Stunt,* is just hitting theaters. As we sit in a windowless room deep in the catacombs of the hockey arena, the heavy pounding of Rush's *Signals* leaks through the walls from the ad-hoc exercise room next door, where keyboardist Kevin Hearn (back in action after winning a battle with leukemia in '98) is doing a preshow workout. Our conversation is interrupted several times by Robertson's gleeful sing-alongs with these anthems of '80s metal, betraying a background that, as Page points out, is practically "a prerequisite for being a Canadian male teenager."

I'd like to go back to the beginning of the Barenaked Ladies duo. Could you set the scene for what a late '80s performance by the two of you was like?

PAGE When we first started playing, I was in the university, and Ed was still in high school. The original gigs we did were all things like playing at our old high school or somebody else's high school—we would just go play at an assembly or something like that. [Our first] real gigs were with this comedy group called Corky and the Juice Pigs. We loved these guys. We saw them and they just killed us—our guts would hurt and our faces would hurt from laughing so much. So Ed bought a four-track recorder, and we made them a tape. They liked it and asked us to open for them on their tour. We had funny stuff on there—by that point we were probably already doing "If I Had $1,000,000," and we did covers of songs like "Wishing Well" by Terence Trent D'Arby with Ed playing acoustic and me playing Casio. We kind of played everything, and basically it was all for laughs, but it also was about the voices singing harmony—that was the greatest rush for us.

But opening for this comedy group, we'd be doing comedy nights at colleges and bars and stuff, and the audience was expecting a comedy act, even though we were never trying to bill ourselves as that. But we certainly learned a lot from Corky and the Juice Pigs about the pacing of the show and how to keep an audience's attention. In a rock club you can just be wallpaper; you can be the sound track to a lifestyle. But a comedy club is like a folk club where you have a captive audience and they are watching and waiting to be entertained, and they'll tell you right away if they're not entertained. So I think it really molded the way we do our show now.

So the whole improv side of what you do was really there from day one.

ROBERTSON That was basically all we had in the beginning.

PAGE Yeah, we didn't have any songs, so it was like, "OK, let's make up songs."

Was it hard to get used to putting yourself out on a limb like that?

ROBERTSON Both of us enjoyed being out on a limb. I was never intimidated by being on stage having no idea what I was about to do, and we kind of reveled in those moments, even when it fell flat. It was like, well at least we went for it. We were just trying to make each other laugh and enjoy the show, and we were never too worried about what anybody thought about it. We had a good time, and I think that's what people gravitated to.

PAGE I think it was just fresh for a lot of people. We were silly and young, and that was half the appeal of it.

ROBERTSON Now we are old and serious, and that's the other half of the appeal.

Did the pop covers you started off doing mold your songwriting as you steered more in that direction?

PAGE Yeah, I think they did. Even though we were an acoustic group rooted in country and folk and whatever else, we were molded by whatever was on the radio. Whether it was Janet Jackson or the Smiths didn't matter; we were just in pursuit of good songs.

ROBERTSON There are a lot of great pop songs—not just Squeeze and the Beatles. The Backstreet Boys have some great pop songs; there are great melodies and great hooks lurking behind synthesizers and drum loops sometimes. Boy bands and girl sensations don't piss me off; what pisses me off is *no* song hidden behind fantastic production. And there's a lot of that right now.

PAGE I think Max Martin, as much as you want to make fun of him or loathe him for being the center of all songwriting right now—he's writing everything from Britney Spears to Backstreet to 'N Sync to Bon Jovi—he writes great songs. He's kind of the Leiber and Stoller of this part of this decade, because he is a controlling force in songwriting. He's writing pop songs that capture a huge part of the population's imagination. Production-wise and presentation-wise, [those artists] are just as disposable as the acts that Goffin and King or any of those kinds of Brill Building writers wrote for in the early '60s.

You mentioned the presentation aspect of music. When you started out, most pop music was so bombastic, and the bands were portrayed with so much self-glamorizing imagery—you know, standing in a barren landscape with black sunglasses on, looking cool and aloof. You steered completely around all of that somehow.

PAGE It didn't make any sense to us. The great thing about the great rock stars, whether it's the Stones or Bowie or the rock stars of today, is that there's a sense of irony and a sense of humor. I thought there was a point in the mid- to late '80s where there was no humor and no irony in self-reflection—it was all about self-aggrandizing qualities. Springsteen ruled the airwaves, and everyone went, "I want to be like that." Springsteen might be the genuine article, but it just kind of begat a lot of posers who weren't of the same quality.

In the past you've mentioned U2 as another example of what you were reacting against.

PAGE I always think of that *Joshua Tree* era of U2. . . . I was a big fan of theirs until that record—it just kind of offended me at my core. In retrospect, it's not a bad record, but I think it summed up a lot about the times that I didn't want to be force-fed. And then when *Rattle and Hum* came out, it was like, "We have just discovered this great thing. It's called *the blues*." And the rest of us in North America were like, "Yeah, we know. It's good." "No, no, we are going to play it, and you're going to love it."

ROBERTSON "No, we're not."

Who were some of your favorite songwriters back in that time?

PAGE I grew up loving the Violent Femmes. Their first and second records were so exciting to me. Gordon Gano wrote that first record when he was about 15. He wasn't looking back on being a teenager and writing about it; he was actually being one and writing astutely and poignantly about it. That blew my mind, along with the energy that that band put out. We were big fans of the Proclaimers. Again, that was rooted in the folk tradition, but it had all the attitude of punk rock. It had this energy and angst and aggressiveness—and tenderness as well.

Billy Bragg was a big thing for us then too. That *Workers Playtime* album was really important to us. I still think it's a great collection of songs, and he was a great performer as well. I remember seeing him as a teenager and saying, "That's what I want to do." I never thought I wanted to be in a band until I saw him play. I had always assumed he was going to be heavy-handed and didactic and try to teach the audience a lesson about politics or something like that, but he did that in his songs, poignantly, and then went on stage and entertained people, related to them. That was a big influence on both of us.

ROBERTSON He was a fantastic performer. When we finished writing and recording *Gordon,* he somehow ended up with a copy of it. He was a big fan and thought that "What a Good Boy" was the best song of the previous couple of years—or whatever he said. And so he invited us over to play his New Year's Eve run of shows in England, which was very exciting for us.

There's a lot of great wordplay in your songs— unusual rhymes and a mixture of sophisticated and everyday language. I saw that Maroon *takes its name from word-jazz poet Ken Nordine, and I was wondering, were there particular people whose use of language inspired you?*

PAGE At that point, I thought They Might Be Giants did that really well, especially on their first two records. I'm trying to think of who else was good at that kind of thing . . .

Take, for example, something like the rhyming of marriage and disparage in the song "Conventioneers." That's a type of language you don't often hear when you're flipping the radio dial.

ROBERTSON We like our two- or three-syllable rhymes.

PAGE They are a little precious for some people, but I always get a kick out of that. . . .
 You know what, the Beastie Boys get away with that like crazy. As far as rhyming skills and jokes and so on, they influenced us a lot.

ROBERTSON I listen to quite a bit of hip-hop and get influenced by the kind of rhyming patterns that they use. It adds a lot to writing pop songs. It can take you away from traditional sorts of patterns, which is kind of cool.

PAGE There is also a Toronto singer-songwriter/guitar player named Kurt Swinghammer who writes a lot like that. "Conventioneers" could be a Kurt Swinghammer song. He is one of those guys we used to see a lot early on who would just blow our minds.

On Maroon, *the pop culture references are subtler than they were in your earlier songs. There's more material like that line from "Off the Hook": "Something that you heard while you were sleeping left you shaken while he stirred." The words just lightly ping the James Bond reference rather than hammering it home. Is that just the way that the songs went on this record, or does it reflect an evolution in your approach to writing?*

PAGE I just think we're more out of the loop culturally now [*laughter*].

ROBERTSON Yeah, I just think Steve and I don't pay any attention to popular sayings.

PAGE *Dissed* is in there.

ROBERTSON *Fly,* being *fly. Chill.*

But there's nothing on Maroon *that has the kind of barrage of pop culture references of a song like "One Week."*

PAGE It's true. A song like "Sell Sell Sell," if it were written a few years ago, would have been packed with concrete references to pop culture. And it just didn't seem to appeal to us in the same way this time. We wanted to write more about the actual experiences rather than just relying on the allusion to explain it. I think that's what we did a lot in the past: use those allusions to pop culture as the keys to the song, as your way to unlock what I am trying to say in that line. But it's kind of an easy way out.

ROBERTSON It's somewhat like printing at the start of a movie, "This is a true story."

PAGE We'd rather do what they did in *Fargo* and say, "This is a true story," and then not make it a true story.

ROBERTSON That's the coolest thing ever.

You say you both were following this new approach in your songwriting; since you work so closely together, do you tend to steer each other in similar directions?

ROBERTSON I think we used to fulfill very definite roles when we started writing together. But we have written together for 12 years now, and we've learned a lot from each other and from the other things that we have done in the meantime. When we write together now, it's a lot more of an ambiguous process. We know each other well enough that I know when Steve is going in a certain direction; he knows when I need help or when to just leave me alone and let me run with something. We know each other's cues.

The process is always different, though. Sometimes Steve will spit out an entire chorus, just like, "I have a chorus idea," and there it is, and it's great. And then other times we are stuck on a single line for 20 minutes.

PAGE With "Conventioneers," one night I came up with the musical part of the song. Ed came by the next day, and it was like, "I've got this idea; I don't know if it's going anywhere." By the time I had finished playing it, I realized that I had all the sections for a song, but we sat down and wrote all the lyrics together.

There were no words yet?

PAGE We didn't even know what it was about. Throughout the songwriting process, we are always saying, "What is this about?" and "Are we getting there?"

ROBERTSON And "Are we saying more than we need to say? Can we be more concise?"

PAGE There's a lot of moving things around, making sure that we are getting the flow of the story or the emotions spaced out properly.

So your ideas are pretty unfinished when you bring them to each other?

PAGE Yeah, and more so on this record. There was a lot of bare-bones stuff that we just sat and wrote together. I think a lot of songwriting partners write the lyrics independently of each other—one guy will write the lyrics, and they'll work on the music together. Or someone will just fill in the music and lyrics for a bridge or a chorus. We've often done that, but this time around it was much more of the two of us writing everything together—and more lyrics than music, which is even rarer.

You are obviously not very proprietary about parts, because one of you might start off writing the guitar part and then the other one winds up performing it, or one of you writes the melody and the other winds up singing it.

ROBERTSON We just want to serve the song, you know?

PAGE With some songs, like "Too Little, Too Late," Ed came up with the musical idea for it, but I ended up singing it. So it makes it sound like it's a Steve song, but they're really all both of ours on this record. And it mashes together somehow. I think part of our strength in writing lyrics together is the fact that we move the song forward in the same way we do it on stage, the same way we complete each other's sentences or continue raps or move the show forward.

ROBERTSON [*Bursts into a sing-along with the Rush album playing next door*] "He's wise enough to win the world but weak enough to lose it. [*Page joins in harmony*] He's a New World man . . ." [*laughter*].

Well, the end result of your songwriting process—

ROBERTSON It's really quite excellent, isn't it, the end result? It's amazing.

What I was going to say is that it's really tight. Do a lot of little pieces and parts wind up on the cutting room floor?

ROBERTSON When we write a song, we combine verses—we'll take the first two lines of one verse and the last two lines of another. We really try to chop the fat from a song.

PAGE The best thing about this record for me is there's nothing that makes me go, "Ooh, that line's still there?" where on other records there are all kinds of lines where I go, "I meant to go back and fix that." We always used to joke, "Oh, we'll go back to that later." It was a joke because we knew we wouldn't. This time we actually did go back later and fix it—the songs are way more airtight than they have been on other records.

ROBERTSON I think it's a great challenge to be concise when writing a song. Any songwriter with a certain degree of experience can get an idea across—it may take five verses or whatever. We challenge ourselves to be really concise and really clear in what we're saying. And that to me is the fun of trying to write a pop song. We want to get 12 of them on the record, and we want them all to be good. And we also try not to repeat ourselves from song to song. If we say, "I think we have already written that in another song," then we try to incorporate what we're working on into that other song.

PAGE That's always the saddest thing in writing songs, when you think, "Oh, we came up with 14 songs, but you know what? This verse would work really well inside this other song."

ROBERTSON Now we have three great songs—we had 14 half songs.

PAGE We are not afraid to merge the songs together to make one better song—take two or three different song ideas, what you think are three different songs, and make them one. It's exciting on the quality level and very sad on the quantity level.

When you get down to the three- or four-minute song, you've obviously thought a lot about the story that is unfolding during that time. You don't just nail the chorus again and again, winding up at the end at the same place where you started.

PAGE They are like short stories. In a short story you've got essentially what happens in a novel in an incredibly condensed form. There is some sense of change—some kind of an epiphany, or an ending that is uplifting or downturning. You don't know where you're going, but you know that you are on a journey that you trust when you're reading. It's the same thing in a song: you trust in the song to take you somewhere that you may or may not expect. [As a songwriter] you are not trying to take advantage of the listener; you're just trying to show a little movie.

ROBERTSON We very definitely write with that movement in mind. We have a very clear idea, even half a verse into a song, of what we want to say and how we want to go about saying it.

For a long time we have been conscious of [the value of] getting together daily and writing, because if you wait for the muse to strike you, there are movies to see and food to eat and places to go. We make sure when it is time to write that we do it every day, and we sit down for four hours. One day we might get half of a verse and another day we might get two songs, but as long as we keep doing it each day, when the muse hits we'll be ready.

That relieves the pressure, too, doesn't it?

PAGE Yeah, if you treat it like a craft. It's like what painters do or authors do: authors sit down at their typewriters, and painters sit down at their easels, every day, and they just write and they just paint. It doesn't have to be good; you just do it, and at the end of the process you can start editing. The editing is a huge part of it. I think people do less and less, just because of the availability of space: 74-minute CDs and Web sites with extra tracks and whatever else.

ROBERTSON People feel like they're getting ripped off if there's not at least 65 minutes of music on the CD. Meanwhile, an LP would hold a maximum of 40, and the last five minutes of each side sounded like crap. You had to be more concise 20 years ago. You had to edit yourself or it didn't fit on the LP. I think there is something great about a record that's under 50 minutes. You should be able to say it in that much time.

Your sound on Maroon *has changed quite a bit from the acoustic guitar and string bass simplicity of* Gordon. *Even in '96, when you recorded* Rock Spectacle, *you were playing almost all acoustic instruments. What has been driving you to add electric instruments to the mix in the last few years?*

ROBERTSON I think just our own interests and exploration into those places. When we made *Gordon,* I was very, "I am an acoustic guitar player—that's what I want to play."

PAGE We were Luddites.

ROBERTSON But we have just been growing in those directions and interested in those sounds. Interesting, when you look around, a lot of that rock energy doesn't necessarily come from big, loud, distorted guitars, and we have just been experimenting with where to find that energy.

PAGE A song like "Falling for the First Time" on this record—which is rock, in some ways the most rocking moment on the record—is driven by acoustic guitar. There's electric in it, but it's a supplemental part. The thrust of it, and what's on the bed track, is the acoustic guitar. So it still is the core of our sound, and "Pinch Me" is an acoustic-driven track, and so forth. It's there, but it has changed.

I think [one influence was] Kevin [Hearn] joining the band in '95. Our old keyboard player, Andy [Creeggan], was really a purist about his keyboard instruments: it had to be either acoustic piano or something like a Rhodes, and that was it. Kevin came with a bunch of synthesizers and a sampler, because that's what he played in his previous band. He brought in all kinds of different textures that we hadn't really imagined in the group before, and I think that opened us up to a lot of different possibilities we hadn't considered previously.

Do you think the band's progression into playing much bigger venues has nudged you to amp up too?

SELECTED DISCOGRAPHY

Maroon, Reprise 47814 (2000).

Stunt, Reprise 46963 (1998).

Rock Spectacle, Reprise 46393 (1996).

Born on a Pirate Ship, Reprise 46128 (1996).

Shoe Box EP, Reprise 46183 (1996).

Maybe You Should Drive, Reprise 45709 (1994).

Gordon, Reprise 26956 (1992).

PAGE Absolutely. When we did our big tour for *Gordon* in Canada in '93, we had an acoustic bass, a piano, some congas, drums, and acoustic guitars. Not a single amplifier on stage except for Jim [Creeggan's bass amp], I guess. It didn't really fill arenas in the same way that a big rock sound does.

Do you find that electric instruments tap into the same sort of instrumental energy that you started with?

ROBERTSON Absolutely. I think right from the beginning we have just been trying to cover a spectrum. We have always been very conscious of what's going on rhythmically and melodically in the song, and of what's going on frequency-wise and sonically between the instruments. We try to keep parts apart so that they're interesting. What I am doing on acoustic guitar isn't stepping on what Jim is doing on bass, and percussion is not overlapping what Tyler is doing. I think we have just translated that formula. You can't just add big, loud guitars; it won't rock all of a sudden. It's about parts. Listen to James Brown, and there is the blueprint for how to do arrangements.

At your sound check, I was listening to you play "Never Do Anything," which you do on electric guitar on the record, but you were playing it on an acoustic, and I was struck by the fact that it sounded basically the same. It had the same sort of drive—the feel is more inherent to the song than to the instrument.

ROBERTSON Yeah, because it is the groove of the part; it's not the sound.

WHAT THEY PLAY (2000)

On Barenaked Ladies' *Maroon* tour, racks of guitars flank both sides of the stage. On Steven Page's side are a row of Guilds: two D-55s, a JF-55-12 12-string (used only for infrequent performances of the song "Helicopters"), and two Blues Bird electrics, one of which is outfitted with a Bigsby bar. A Telecaster rounds out the collection. The acoustics are amplified with Fishman Matrix Natural pickups run through a Nady wireless system and a Countryman DI—and no other effects. "The more no-frills, the better," posits Page; his and Robertson's guitar techs agree emphatically that on-board preamps and such only increase the odds of gear "voodoo," and sonic nuances can be more than handled elsewhere when you travel with a $90,000 monitor console.

At home, Page has an array of other guitars, including Guild Starfire hollow-body electrics, a '70s Les Paul, and a small-body, all-mahogany Martin from 1930. "I love it," he says of the vintage Martin. "I got it six years ago, and I have never changed the strings. I don't want to jinx it now. It doesn't tune great, but it sounds really cool. I've also got a small Taylor that I use as a high-string guitar. I just got a National steel, and I am going to use that for home recordings and such." Page uses a Dunlop clamp-type capo and Dean Markley strings: on the acoustics, a medium-light set (.012 to .054), and on the electrics, a custom set of .011, .014, plain .020, .030, .038, and .050. "I used to play a wound .020, but essentially because I wasn't a very good guitar player, I would end up bending the G string every time. I was trying to find something that was heavier in the B and G area."

Ed Robertson's stage acoustics are two copies of his treasured 1976 Larrivée L-09, which he recently retired from the road and uses only in the studio. His acoustics are amplified similarly to Page's, with a Fishman Matrix Natural pickup running through a Shure wireless system and a Demeter tube direct box. Both guitarists use feedback-busting soundhole covers, which they remove when they do their frequent "busking sets" at radio stations, stores, and other makeshift settings.

Robertson's expanding collection of electric guitars includes several instruments by New York—area luthier Dennis Fano, who also builds guitars for XTC and other rockers. Filling out the rack are solid- and hollow-bodies by Paul Reed Smith, Fender, and Gibson. Robertson uses Shubb capos and, like Page, Dean Markley strings: medium-lights on the acoustics and a heavy bottom/light top set on the electrics (.010 to .052).

In keeping with their seat-of-the-pants performing philosophy, Page and Robertson take the inevitable gear problems in stride—like the acoustic pickup blowup that recently occurred in front of an audience of 40,000. "I always catch myself when something goes wrong. It's like, why should I really care?" says Page. "If some guitar blows up, it's shrug and move on, make a joke of it. If anybody can make a bad situation work, it's us. It actually fuels us; it makes us play better too."

PAGE Also, a lot of what we do on records is take an electric guitar part and then double it with an acoustic guitar, or with the Dobro on songs like "One Week."

There's also some stuff on the record where you go beyond the sounds of guitar, like "Tonight Is the Night I Fell Asleep at the Wheel."

PAGE We found guitar on that song wasn't working; we couldn't get it to fit in that soundscape. So Ed played the banjo on that track instead.

ROBERTSON Because I am an excellent banjo player [*laughs*]. I played a six-string banjo tuned like a guitar. I am trying to learn to play banjo, but I am not particularly excellent yet. I am working on it. I can play "Cripple Creek"—not [*sings*] "Up on Cripple Creek, she sends me," but [*hums fiddle tune*].

PAGE Watch out, Tony Trischka.

Your songs often have these interesting internal contradictions—things pulling in opposite directions. For instance, "Pinch Me" has upbeat, light-sounding music, but the words are about a very serious, grown-up kind of philosophical questioning, and then thrown in the middle you have the bit of classic kid humor in the lines "I could hide out under there / I just made you say underwear." Do these kinds of juxtapositions come from a very highly developed sense of mischief?

PAGE Yeah. Some people think things like the underwear line rip off the song, like we can't afford to be serious long enough. But for us, it's just about who we are and how we talk, and about finding humor in mundane things.

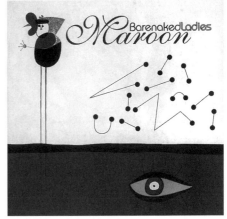

ROBERTSON That's the way I relate to the world. In those dire, depressing times, I do look for the smile in the situation—not to make it go away, but to cope with it. I have always approached life like that, and so those lines in those songs are more to emphasize the cloud inside the silver lining. I think it only serves to illustrate the direness of the situation. If I am cracking jokes about it, I am trying to cheer myself up.

ANI DIFRANCO

Ani DiFranco is one of the most potent and prolific artists to emerge from the post–baby boom generation, a galvanizing force on musicians of many stripes both for her principled independence in the music business and for her boundless creativity. She appears here in two encounters: first in 1997 in the company of legendary singer/story-teller/rabble-rouser Utah Phillips, with whom she had just created an extraordinary album, *The Past Didn't Go Anywhere* (the success of that project inspired another collaboration, *Fellow Workers,* in 1999); then by herself in 2000, during a band tour following the release of her album *To the Teeth*. These two conversations reveal different sides of her—the former focuses on roots and politics, while the latter peers inside her creative process—but her values and passions are consistent. She has such a strong presence that it is a little jarring to meet her in person; her diminutive frame and disarmingly sweet, thoughtful manner are the polar opposite of what we expect in the rock world's parade of egos.

RADICAL FOLK

"People my age find folk music very uncool—it's just terribly, terribly uncool," says Ani DiFranco. With her cropped, green hair, boy's hockey jersey, collarbone tattoo, and spiked leather jacket with a sticker on the back that says "Mean People Suck," DiFranco hardly looks like most people's idea of a folkie—and her edgy, often frenetic music doesn't sound much like most people's idea of folk, either. So what is she doing here in Toronto at the Folk Alliance conference, an annual gathering of the faithful presided over by such archetypal folksingers as Pete Seeger? DiFranco is here because she has her own definition of the *f* word. "Folk music is not an acoustic guitar—that's not where the heart of it is," she says. "I use the word *folk* in reference to punk music and to rap music. It's an attitude, it's an awareness of one's heritage, and it's a community. It's subcorporate music that gives voice to different communities and their struggle against authority."

The fact that DiFranco defines folk by its spirit and intent rather than its sound and dress code goes a long way toward explaining her connection with Utah Phillips, the venerable singer and storyteller who sits next to her in this hotel ballroom. From his fedora and snow-white beard to his repertoire of labor songs and populist anthems, Phillips is as unambiguously a folksinger as he could be—and as stylistically distant from DiFranco as he could be. But appearances are deceiving. Just a few hours ago, DiFranco helped present Phillips with Folk Alliance's Lifetime Achievement Award, citing his gift for entwining humor, entertainment, and politics as an inspiration for her own music. This is only one of the many traits and passions they share; their connection is so strong, in fact, that he's the first outside artist DiFranco has brought onto the roster of her own Righteous Babe Records label.

DiFranco's and Phillips' 1996 album for Righteous Babe, *The Past Didn't Go Anywhere*, is much more than a unique collaboration between a folk elder and a rising young star; it's a bold and ambitious musical statement, brilliantly executed. DiFranco sifted through 100 hours of

Phillips' live tapes and picked a handful of her favorite between-song raps—the ones that, she says, "made me fall off my chair laughing or just go off in the corner and cry and mull things over for a while." She then took those stories—chronicling Phillips' desertion from the army during the Korean War, the mentors who taught him about politics and life, and various philosophical observations from his years on the road and rail—and holed up in an Austin studio to layer music tracks beneath them. Primarily using light funk and hip-hop rhythms, with dashes of guitar and other instruments, DiFranco created a completely different musical context for Phillips' words while preserving their soul—making a sort of end run around people's stereotypes of folk music.

"It was a very calculated move on my part," says DiFranco, "because I can see people around me, people my age, who haven't had the experience I have of being thrown into folk festivals half their lives and coming into contact with all this crazy, subcorporate music. I think that they'd be people who'd see Utah and think, 'What is this? He looks like Santa Claus, he's sitting on a stool with an acoustic guitar, and he's singing, what, labor songs? This has nothing to do with me. I don't think so. No—see ya.' They would never find out that what he has to say *does* have something to do with them. So [the album] was taking Utah and putting him into a different context that somebody my age does have a vocabulary for, and then getting them to hear what he has to say."

For his part, Phillips confesses that when DiFranco originally proposed the project, he had no idea what the result might be like. So, did the radically new medium for his message come as a shock? "I thought it was marvelous," Phillips says. "If I were to pick stories that I wanted to persist if I weren't around, those are the ones I would pick. Not only that, but she put them in the right order. That's real judgment, almost instinctive. I have old folk music friends, older people, who say, 'Gee, I wish your voice was louder and the music was softer.' I just say, 'Hey, this wasn't made for you.'" He adds with a laugh, "Sometimes it's hard for people to believe that there's something in the world that wasn't made for them."

The stories collected on *The Past Didn't Go Anywhere* are amazing creations—folksy and literary at the same time, alternately playful, piercing, mischievous, and nostalgic. A true wordsmith, Phillips is always up to more than he lets on. "I always believed that what happened between the songs was as important as the songs," he says. "I put a lot of time into the stories, so that people would laugh and we would share absurdities together; and I would create this little, narrow window where I could deal with the labor movement, where I could deal with pacifism, whatever it was that I was there to do—my agenda—without being ghettoized as a political performer.

"You talked to me in one of your letters about it," he says to DiFranco. "You said, 'I understand the use of humor in performance. You've got to get people laughing so their throats open up wide enough to be able to swallow something bigger.' That struck me. First of all, it's funny, and it's a very true thing to say."

The process by which DiFranco married Phillips' words with music was entirely improvisational. "I would start with the story," she says. "I would find the BPM [beats per minute] of the story and try to negotiate a rhythm track to it, and then I would usually start with the bass. I've got an old Fender P. [Precision] bass. I would come up with a bass line and then build on top of that." From story to story, DiFranco's music varies to match the mood. For the lighthearted satire of "Nevada City, California," she set up Phillips' punch lines with stop-and-start funk rhythms, as in an old *Laugh-In* sketch. In the elegiac "Half a Ghost Town," the music pares down to a slow, sad melody played on a tenor guitar. One of the most haunting moments comes in "Korea," when the sound of Phillips tuning his guitar—one of the few appearances of his guitar on the record—becomes a ghostly melody floating above the loping beat. "The sound of him tuning the guitar became this kind of trance to me," says DiFranco. "I sampled that bit of tuning and sort of made the melodic structure around that."

It's impossible to listen to the words of Utah Phillips without conjuring an image of him on stage: the raconteur and folk historian, singing and strumming and spinning yarns for an audience. The tradition of folk music he carries on has a clear public purpose—it's really inconceivable without an audience. This would seem to be a major difference between him and DiFranco, who was born into the singer-songwriter age, which values introspection over social commentary and writing your own songs over learning any tradition. But here, again, appearances are deceiving. "I don't think with either one of us it's either/or," says Phillips of the contrast between outward-looking and inward-looking music. "It flows back and forth as a pulse, as a sensibility. Woody Guthrie wrote, 'When I was walking that endless highway'—there's a lot of *I* in Woody. Even when he was writing about someone else, he would still transpose it into the first person, as he took these journeys into himself. I can't fault that and say that's primarily ego-driven. What I think *you're* talking about is music which is ego-driven, what you would call journal-entry songwriting. That's not what Ani does, the way that I hear it. I know that's not what I do, [which is to] let people know that I'm alive and present, and this is how I'm authentically perceiving and thinking, but to expand it to the point where it can take in a lot of what other people are experiencing."

"That whole introspective singer-songwriter thing has been kind of foisted on me," DiFranco adds. "Some people perceive what I do in that way because I write songs through my own experience. But whenever people say, 'Well, your work is very confessional,' I say, 'It's not confessional. I'm not confessing anything. I haven't sinned. These are not my secrets. This is just my life; this is the stuff I've seen, the stuff I did, and what I thought about.' There are different ways of speaking your political perceptions, and it may be [talking about] an event that occurred in your life or an event that occurred in your town . . . but each is a valid path to a certain realization. I think that what we both do is very much about our small, little epiphanies along the way, moments of connection between things."

DiFranco with Utah Phillips.

The introspective tag, DiFranco feels, is often mistakenly applied to the work of women songwriters. "Women have not been all that instrumental in making and running governments and businesses," she says, "and when we sing our labor songs, it's like, we're at home. In a historical perspective, women's politics exist more in terms of human interrelationships, which is what we've been assigned to take care of in society. People look at a chick singing about her abortion or her relationships and think, 'Oh, that's hyperconfessional, personal,' but to me it's all political. It's all related."

To DiFranco and Phillips, performing music is all about making that connection between the individual and the group. "When Utah's singing a labor song," she says, "the people who work in that town are coming up and saying, 'Yeah, me too. I can't believe you said that.'"

"Yeah, you get that too," Phillips responds.

"Absolutely," says DiFranco. "Except for me, I'm up there singing my songs, and who comes up? It's young women in droves: 'Yeah, I can't believe you said that.' It's the same thing: giving voice to different groups of people."

Utah Phillips takes his role as a community voice very seriously. In fact, he's made a life's work of learning music and stories from people, starting back in the early '50s with a job on a road crew and some songs by Jimmie Rodgers and Hank Snow. "The guys on the road crew were the ones who taught me to play the guitar and sing those songs," he says. "But it turned out that the songs weren't the important part—the people who taught them to me were the important part. I can't remember those songs, but I can remember those people."

When DiFranco was first delving into music as a kid in the '70s, the typical way to learn was through recordings, copping songs and licks from pop LPs. Was this her experience? Not at all, she says. "I definitely learned how to play guitar from people. My parents didn't have a record player, so my whole experience with music was made by people in the room for most of my formative years. Luckily for me, there were always a lot of people around playing guitar, and so [music] has always been something you *did*, not something you bought. I didn't idolize rock stars, I didn't have wet dreams about . . . whoever; I just had friends who were teaching me songs. I never really aspired to that rock-star thing; it was a party."

Perhaps because of her record-free childhood, DiFranco also never adopted the common belief that recording is the most important work of a professional musician and performing is a secondary consideration.

Phillips notes, "Too many young people are getting that backward, that somehow a recording history is going to make a living for you. It's not. What would Bob Feldman from Red House Records tell you, or Ken [Irwin] from Rounder? They'd say, 'For us to put out a record of you, you've got to be doing at least 100 dates a year. Otherwise it's not worth it.'"

DiFranco says, "Kids come up to me, and they want advice about what's the magic formula to get the national tours and the distribution. You can see they want, want, want all these things. And I think, 'Maybe you should just try to get a gig. Maybe you should just get a gig, and then maybe you should do that every weekend for ten years, and then see if you're not on a haphazard national tour that grew organically and if you don't have some recordings that you made along the way that are distributed through the people you encountered along the way.'"

"What's the work of a poet?" Phillips adds. "To write poetry. What's the work of an artist? To paint. What's the work of a singer? To sing. I tell them, 'Fasten totally on the work. Give yourself completely to the work, till you can do it as well as it can be done, and then people will come looking for you. But forget the rest of it. That will happen if you're completely fixed on the work.'"

That phrase *the work* keeps popping up in conversation with these two, who hold an entirely down-to-earth view of what it means to be a musician. "What mass media have done to the entertainer in this culture is beyond description," says Phillips, "to the point where you could have a panel of a world expert on nutrition and a sitcom star next to each other, and they would quote and listen to the sitcom star, as if their opinion was more valuable than this person's who has spent their life studying something. We've really inflated the role of the entertainer in this society, instead of looking at the entertainer as I think we must look at ourselves: as simply good carpenters, good plumbers. Who isn't afraid of bad carpentry? Who isn't afraid of bad plumbing? As artists, we're not any more or any less than trying to become journeymen, journeywomen, at a trade, after an apprenticeship, and then to do that for an adequate compensation so that we can get through in the world. Why must it be anything greater than that?

"That's a very deep mystery to me, how we let that get out of control, how we let that happen. Because in antiquity, even on the frontier in America, people sang and did poems and dances as an organic part of their lives. You went from the threshing floor to the dance floor easily. What happened that made those who could play and those who could sing special people? More than special people—we turned them into idols, turned them into gods."

DiFranco and Phillips may feel that performing is their true calling, and that recording is a by-product, but there's a rich irony behind that sentiment: their collaboration would never have happened without recording technology. *The Past Didn't Go Anywhere* is a studio-created illusion, a technological bridge between far-distant musical styles. Plus, individually, they *are* recording artists; DiFranco in particular has been making records at a breakneck pace. If, as she suggests, the fixation on recordings and product is one of the main characteristics of commercial music that distinguish it from folk music like hers and Phillips', how do these two deal in the record business without losing touch with the wellsprings of their music?

The answer is unanimous: by maintaining a fiercely independent stance vis-à-vis the corporate music business. That's a serious understatement when referring to a man who is fond of saying things such as, "Capitalism is a criminal conspiracy to divest those who do the work of the wealth that they create," and a woman who sings (no, *screams*) at corporate America, "I'm the million you never made" and has become the poster child for DIY musicians. Still, I decide to play devil's advocate and ask them: Couldn't you deliver the same messages that you put out there as a performer now while being part of the corporate music world?

"Not a chance," says Phillips. "It would destroy your soul. I would rather sleep under a railroad bridge than work for these assholes. No, sir, you've got to own the means of production. You've got to own what you do.

"If you create it, you're not going to wait around for some big company to sign you to a label. [*To DiFranco*] you created a label. Kate Wolf did that when she created Owl Records. She didn't wait around to be invited to a folk festival; she created one—the Sonoma Folk Festival. You don't wait around for these people to acknowledge you. Meanwhile, sure, you make less, you learn to live cheap, you really learn to find your wants and needs in a sensible fashion. It's like an indentured servant buying himself out from indenture, from capitalism. *But,* at a subindustrial level, you make all the artistic decisions—not the people in the front office, not the people who try to shape your image—and that's what keeps the material flowing and fresh. When you give in to their system, when you become a bought person and they're going to give you wealth, power, and fame, and the creative decisions are then being made more and more by the people in the front office, all you can begin to write about is your personal sense of alienation. You think over the careers of the singer-songwriters of the '60s and '70s, and that's what you hear."

"And what you have to say will become, without a doubt, systematically watered down to be more radio-friendly and to be more accessible," DiFranco adds. "They come up with all kinds of convincing arguments about why you should adjust your image or why you should play *this* song every time you appear on TV and water down any kind of political implications in your music, so that you can be accessible and make the biggest buck."

Take control and take responsibility: this credo runs deep in DiFranco and Phillips, guiding much more than just their careers. It's a philosophy of life that Phillips traces to his mentor Ammon Hennacy, described on *The Past Didn't Go Anywhere* as a "Catholic, anarchist, pacifist, draft dodger of two world wars, tax refuser, vegetarian, one-man revolution in America." Phillips says, "My body is my ballot, and I try to cast it on behalf of the people around me every day of my life. I accept the responsibility to make sure that things get done. I love to tell that to people who are frustrated with the ballot box. How many people do I know who have never voted for anyone who won, and are really frustrated? It's not the end of the road. There's another way to go, and that's with your own labor, your own sweat, your own body. I think there's a lot of hope in that."

In the liner notes to *The Long Memory,* the 1996 album by Phillips and Rosalie Sorrels, he wrote, "The long memory is the most radical idea in the country. It is the loss of that long memory which deprives our people of that connective flow of thoughts and events that clarifies our vision, not of where we're going but where we want to go." Phillips' mission is to be a vehicle for that memory, a means by which important ideas, stories, and aspirations are passed from generation to generation. "I'm just a folksinger," he says, "but I have a thorough understanding of what that means. Growing up means at some point in your life discovering what you culturally inherit. You finally recognize that, and that's what you try to put in the world. And that's what I do now. I find that my inheritance is a wealth of song and story and poem from my elders—especially the radical elders, who never had that wide a voice in their lives."

In creating *The Past Didn't Go Anywhere,* DiFranco aims to be another link in that chain. "The pop music realm has a huge disrespect for our elders," she says. "It's all about worshipping youth. Youth has a lot of energy, and there's a lot of important shit that goes down in youth culture, but I don't think that means you ignore your elders or where you come from. People may constantly want to be inventing the new alternative, which so quickly gets co-opted and turned into just a cookie-cutter formula, with just a slightly more distorted guitar or something, whereas they might be ignoring the fact that they could take the same old tools— an acoustic guitar—and be working in an old, crusty medium like folk music, and do something totally new.

"Like Utah would say, 'Shut up and listen to what came before you and see what use it has.'"

INSIDE THE MUSIC

The new singer-songwriter generation. The rise of acoustic rock. Artists go indie. Radical alternate tunings. Two-handed tapping. Pushing the acoustic-electric envelope. These were some of the forces that changed the face of acoustic music and the guitar in the '90s, and they can all be neatly evoked with just two words: Ani DiFranco.

With 14 solo albums, hundreds upon hundreds of gigs, and numerous genre-bending collaborations (with Utah Phillips, saxman Maceo Parker, Prince . . .) during the last decade, DiFranco was an artistic force to be reckoned with. And now she's roaring into the '00s with her best album yet (*To the Teeth*), a new band spiced with New Orleans–inspired horns, and, as usual, enough projects and schemes to occupy six musicians with normal metabolisms. (To name a few: a Woody Guthrie collection, *'Til We Outnumber 'Em,* featuring Bruce Springsteen, Indigo Girls, and others; an album by the duo Bitch and Animal; and the launch of Righteous Babe Books.) DiFranco's latest songs are deeper, funkier, and more piercingly honest than ever, and her guitar work on acoustic, tenor, baritone, and electric shows the touch of a true master, although it has shifted toward the background with the expansion of her band.

Curiously, though, DiFranco's spectacular success in running her own label (2.5 million albums sold to date), coupled with her forthright, intelligent, and eminently quotable views about maintaining artistic integrity in the age of mega-corporations, has put her much more in the spotlight as the indie-label poster girl than as one of the defining artistic voices of our time. To shed some light on the techniques and inspirations behind her music, she met with me for an afternoon conversation backstage at the Luther Burbank Center in Santa Rosa, California, where her young fans had already been camped out for hours in anticipation of the evening's show. In a room queasily decorated like the inside of a disco-era van, DiFranco succeeded in cracking open a window for a blast of fresh air, then sat down and offered these thoughts on the state of her music ten

years after starting Righteous Babe Records and bursting out of the folk scene like a ball of fire.

Revisiting your debut album recently, I was struck by a statement you made in the liner notes: "I speak without reservation from what I know and who I am. I do so with the understanding that all people should have the right to offer their voice to the chorus, whether the result is harmony or dissonance. The worldsong is a colorless dirge without the differences which distinguish us, and it is that difference which should be celebrated, not condemned. Should any part of my music offend you, please do not close your ears to it; just take what you can use and move on." Do you recall what was going through your mind when you wrote that?

DIFRANCO Oh yeah, it went through my mind every day for years and years. I encountered so much resistance back in the early days. I started writing songs when I was 14 or something, but by the time I made that first record, I had been playing out, just beginning to get on the folk circuit and going to colleges around the Northeast. There wasn't a lot of cultural precedent for women singing about their lives. My songs were informed by my life, my gender, my identity, and that seemed to have no place in the world around me. Like my anger, for instance: if I included that in my songs, in my vocabulary of emotions, I seemed to get a lot of defensive reactions.

The audiences that I played to were much more polarized than they are now. The people who really embraced what I was saying and understood it were other young women, and then there was this whole contingent

that [treated me as if] I were some kind of in-your-face, angry, screaming thrash band or something. I spent a lot of time on stage trying to convince people that no, I'm not an angry person, I just have opinions, and it's not demeaning to you for me to talk about my experience.

Did putting out a record feel like stepping into a much more public forum than performing?

DIFRANCO No, it didn't feel like that at all. For me the stage is an immediate, visceral, highly exposed, vulnerable place, and making a record is kind of vicarious. It never had the impact for me that performing does. But because the albums have lives of their own, I learned that recording things is much more exposing than being on stage for a fleeting moment. It's this terrible, stagnant eternity of recorded music.

Did some of the reactions you got come from addressing topics that people were just not ready to hear someone sing about?

DIFRANCO Yeah. You know, I was singing about an abortion I had when I was 18, I was singing about sexual identity and the fluidity of that in my experience, and singing about power dynamics between men and women, and I would get these ridiculous responses. Middle-aged men would come up to me after a folk festival workshop and say, "Well, you know, men are not all bad," or something like that, and I'd be like, "Oh really? What a subtle interpretation of the song I just played." But it taught me a lot about the society around me, because I was writing these little songs and they were like cultural litmus tests. Anyone of any sex, age, make, or model could position themselves anywhere in the song.

Did anyone in particular light the fire in you to put your perspective out there?

DIFRANCO I think I was just born with that fire. Inspiration has come from so many places, but that unquenchable need to express and communicate was an inherent thing. But back in the day, there were also a lot of people who were really supportive and welcoming, people like Tom Paxton or Utah Phillips or Greg Brown, or people who were just immediately like, "Yeah, welcome, shake it up." That sense of community I started to experience pretty early on was very inspiring and helped me to sustain myself, even just emotionally, out there alone, driving along from folk club to folk club, just knowing that I'm not the only one who does that.

Your guitar playing sounded very different on your debut than it does now. You did a lot more traditional fingerpicking and not so much with tunings and percussion. How did your style evolve?

DIFRANCO There are so many factors. I learned how to play guitar with folk fingerpicking, but after years of playing solo in clubs and bars, I was learning to be my own rhythm section and starting to incorporate bass lines into my guitar parts. Fingerpicking is this direct relationship between rhythm and melody—that's the incredible thing about the guitar, and my acoustic guitar taught me everything I know about music. It's a percussion instrument, for sure, but every beat has a note to it, so that relationship became more and more intriguing to me, and the rhythm of the guitar part just became more and more primary in my consciousness. When I started playing with a band, I started trying to steer what was going on through the guitar. Over the years of playing with other musicians my playing just got tighter and tighter, and sparser and sparser, because I so much love the spaces in music.

These days, you're often riding on top of the other instruments, laying back more than you used to.

DIFRANCO Now that I have a band that I love, we have a developing musical relationship that is so exciting, but I do play a lot less. On *Out of Range* or *Not a Pretty Girl* or before I started touring full-time with a band, I was getting my ya-ya's out on the guitar a lot more, and I miss that. I just went on a little solo tour a couple weeks ago, and that was fun to get back to being my own band.

Have alternate tunings been part of your playing for a long time?

DIFRANCO Yeah, for a long time. The only tuning that I learned was D A D G A D, back in the day, and now I have a hundred little permutations of different tuning families. It's all born of sitting around with my guitar looking for a new palette of colors.

Are you aware of the notes when you retune?

DIFRANCO Not all the time. . . . I've been throwing in a lot of C's these days. I really like the sound of two C's on top—B string up and E string way down, and maybe a C or a D on the bottom. I've also got a lot of tunings now with a pile of G's in them.

Some of your tunings go really low, like the song "Swing" from To the Teeth.

DIFRANCO That's actually on a baritone guitar, which I've been playing more these days.

You're also playing a lot of tenor guitar. Did you gravitate to these instruments by just searching for sounds?

DIFRANCO The tenor guitar came to me from Scott [Freilich], who has a guitar shop in Buffalo [Top Shelf Music]. I've known him since I was 15— he was in my band when I was a teenager. He specializes in antique instruments and whatnot, and every now and then he'll call me up and say, "I have this sweet beast in my shop you might want to check out." Many years ago he put this tenor guitar in my hands and I fell in love with it. And then I have such a fetish for a punchy, big, round, beefy acoustic guitar sound, I started thinking, maybe I'm playing the wrong instrument. Maybe I should be playing a baritone acoustic. So I checked out a bunch of baritone guitars, and now I have one of those Danelectro reissue electric baritones, which is a really beautiful thing.

You're playing acoustic baritone, too.

DIFRANCO Yeah, most of the time. It's an Alvarez, and it's really sweet.

Are you still playing the Alvarez Bob Weir model you've been using for years?

DIFRANCO Yeah. I have a relationship with them now, and they help me out, because I tend to beat my guitars to hell. I mean I love them, I don't intentionally hurt them at all, but I claw through the faces and break braces. My guitar tech, Reg [Dickinson], has become like this mad scientist, and he's constantly messing with the intonation, tweaking the preamp, replacing the pickup, trying different gauge strings. . . . We're in a constant dialogue.

So you get into that tech stuff, too?

DIFRANCO Oh yeah! You know, my whole life is the way that guitar sounds coming back through the monitors.

Some musicians have no head for that kind of thing—they just want to plug and play.

DIFRANCO I'm so jealous of those people! Greg Brown, for instance, brilliant songwriter, stands up on stage, plugs it in, "OK, seems good," not feeding back. Being at liberty to just play, and not to be microscopically aware of the tone of your instrument all the time, it must be so fabulous. But me, I subject myself and some other very unfortunate people to excruciating sound checks. But I'm also trying to get my instrument to do something it's not really designed to do. And I hate that scratchy, tinny acoustic guitar business.

Do you still like to overdrive the acoustic for distortion and other effects?

DIFRANCO Oh yeah. All my guitars run through a wah pedal that has a little switch that's off unless I go for it. And they all run through a little amp so I can add crunch now and then. On record, a lot of the time, I'll mic the guitar in a couple places and take the pickup direct—oftentimes punchiness in the bass is what I'll use that [pickup] channel for. And then I send it to an amp, so I can get kind of a shifting guitar sound from just playing one track.

You've obviously done a lot of experimenting in the studio.

DIFRANCO Well, you sit behind a board for enough years and you start turning knobs—either that or you fall asleep. I've always made my own records, so it's been a really deep learning slope for me, but it's all about figuring out how to use my ears and how to use gear to satisfy my ears.

Had you done much recording before your first album?

DIFRANCO Yeah, little cassettes before then or whatnot. But the first album was recorded in just a couple of hours with two microphones, direct to DAT. Then there was a bunch of years of recording in cheesy Buffalo or Toronto studios with long-haired metal guys, people who didn't necessarily have ears for acoustic music. And I'm just there all alone, without any conception of what an acoustic guitar should sound like or what I'm going for, just complete ignorance. So there were many albums that reflect mostly on the engineers' sensibilities that I was working with. It took me a good ten records before I started to have an aesthetic at all.

On which album did that kick in? Little Plastic Castle?

DIFRANCO Before that. It's a very gradual process. I started to move in the direction of my own sound with *Out of Range, Not a Pretty Girl*—I can hear the beginnings of an idea. With *Dilate*, I was completely alone in the studio for most of that mixing process, and I was also just in a really bad mood. I was working in this studio without any kind of subwoofer, and I'd had the worst year of my life, and I was making this punishing album of "I just want to put my head in a hole" songs and not even hearing what I'm doing on the low end. So it's this colossal record of *buffing* bass.

You've been recording at an incredible rate over the last ten years. These days, how long do you typically spend making a record?

DIFRANCO A couple weeks. I can't spend a lot of time in the studio. A few weeks ago I was on tour with Gillian Welch and Greg Brown, and I was talking to Gillian and David [Rawlings], the dynamic duo, about their two records, and I was flabbergasted at the amount of money and time that they spent in the studio. For their first record, they spent six weeks in the studio.

And it's almost all just two guitars and two voices—

DIFRANCO —and all you have to do is sit them down and press record and there's the song. It's not like there's any kind of tomfoolery going on those records. And I was like, what do you do for six weeks? That whole culture of perfection, I have no patience for that. Making music is so immediate, and the fact that there's no audience in the studio is a hurdle for me to begin with. I just can't sit around and try and make the perfect vocal and the perfect guitar track. I lose artistic inspiration for that kind of obsessiveness. So what I've learned to do these days, starting with the *Up Up Up* record, is to record a bunch of different times, because the song as you play it on any given day is just that day's interpretation. I thought, "OK, if I can't sit for a week and think about a song in the studio and play it a hundred times, then maybe I could record a bunch of songs this week, record all those same songs four months later, somewhere else, and then do it again three months later." We recorded *To the Teeth* over the course of three- to seven-day snatches, and a lot of stuff I recorded myself in the timelessness of the wee hours over the course of a year. Then you have a few different versions that happen in the moment, but you can put them against each other and say, "OK, this one sounds most like the song, and that one, I don't know what we were on that day."

DISCOGRAPHY

To the Teeth, Righteous Babe 17 (1999).
Fellow Workers (with Utah Phillips), Righteous Babe 15 (1999).
Little Plastic Remixes (vinyl EP), Righteous Babe 14 (1999).
Up Up Up Up Up Up, Righteous Babe 13 (1999).
Little Plastic Castle, Righteous Babe 12 (1998).
Living in Clip, Righteous Babe 11 (1997).
More Joy, Less Shame (CD EP), Righteous Babe 10 (1996).
The Past Didn't Go Anywhere (with Utah Phillips), Righteous Babe 9 (1996).
Dilate, Righteous Babe 8 (1996).
Not a Pretty Girl, Righteous Babe 7 (1995).
Out of Range, Righteous Babe 6 (1994).
Like I Said: Songs 1990–91, Righteous Babe 5 (1993).
Puddle Dive, Righteous Babe 4 (1993).
Imperfectly, Righteous Babe 3 (1992).
Not So Soft, Righteous Babe 2 (1991).
Ani DiFranco, Righteous Babe 1 (1990).

When I look at the amount of recording you do, the amount of touring you do, plus the label and all the other projects, it seems impossible that you would have the kind of concentrated time you need for writing songs. How do you do that?

DIFRANCO Just eliminating sleep, basically . . . I see the sunrise most mornings. People have always asked me that, and I never really knew the answer, except I'm beginning to realize that it's that time I spend lying awake all night. Like last night, this morning, I saw the sunrise and then I got into my little bunk, my little coffin on the bus, and I couldn't sleep and I sort of catnapped until about 11:30. Then I got up because all I could think of was, I have two new people in my band, horn section, and I have all of these specific suggestions about what people are playing, and then kind of theoretical things I want to try to express to bring us closer, to keep us listening more and more. So I was lying awake having conversations in my head with my band members, and then I was thinking about albums I'm gonna record soon. There's just so much subconscious work that I have to do when I'm not literally working.

So you can get into that creative mode, wherever you may be.

DIFRANCO Because of the chaos and the velocity of my life nowadays, I've had to learn how to write and whatnot on the road. I was just down in the dressing room working on a little riff and an idea for a new song. I used to be much more precious about it; I used to have to be alone, completely alone, in my own space and sometimes for days before I could really start to talk to myself. But now as my life has gotten ridiculous, I've consciously taught myself to sit in a corner, facing a wall, and work on a lick while everybody's horsing around in the dressing room or shaving heads. I'll chat with them but try to find my own headspace too. But it's really claustrophobic sometimes. I covet my time alone; that's very rare. I would like to do more decompressing and more writing, but I also get such gratification and such inspiration from [all the activity]. It's this catch-22 of creating and doing.

Do you write a lot more music than you actually perform or record?

DIFRANCO Yeah. We have a studio in our little house. I got hitched to my engineer—he does the stage sound, monitors, on tour—and when we go home what he loves to do is watch little levels on preamps and plug in microphones, and what I love to do is make sounds, so we're this symbiotic little force. Whenever we go home now we're recording. I'll just pick something up and he'll stick a mic in front of it. Most of the time he doesn't know, are we making a record or are we having fun? I'll clue him in at some point as to what I think I'm doing.

How much space does the label take up in your head while you're doing all these other things?

DIFRANCO I have to be conscious of it, but I'm at a very good place these days where something crazy like 15 people work at the label, very instrumental people like Scot Fisher, my manager, who's the president of the record company and runs the joint and has for years. He is much more the day-to-day creator of Righteous Babe Records than I am. I'm the idea and the energy behind it, and he's the one who really makes it happen. Without him, I'd still be selling tapes out of the trunk of my car. So I have the luxury of coming up with ideas like making a record with Utah Phillips and then be able to realize that idea with the help of all the people at the label. They'll get behind it and oversee a lot of things like the jungle of printing and manufacturing, distribution, and all of those things that I have no mind for. It has also given me this mechanism to do political work using the resources of the company.

Do you still get down into every detail of the CD artwork and such?

DIFRANCO Oh yeah. Actually, for our new record of Woody Guthrie songs, the artwork was designed by a real graphic designer. We found somebody who does that for a living! It's so funny to me, because I think a lot of people have this impression that I'm a colossal control freak, that I have to do everything myself. But [in reality], once you make the decision that you're not going to work for a corporation and you still want to make music, there's nobody else around to do all of that stuff, and for years I've coveted the help of, for instance, a graphic designer. It's only recently

DIFRANCO DETUNES

Guitar tech Reg Dickinson estimates that three-quarters of Ani DiFranco's repertoire strays from standard tuning, and he provided this sampling of tunings for songs in her current live show.

STANDARD "Out of Habit," "Providence," "Gravel"

E A D G B C "Back Back Back"

C F B♭ E♭ G C (standard lowered two whole steps, baritone guitar) "Wish I May," "I Know This Bar," "Swing"

A♭ F B♭ E♭ G C (baritone guitar) "Reckoning"

C A D G C C "So What" (unreleased song)

A A D G A D (.070 bass string) "Dilate"

E B B G A D (capo II) "Shy"

E B B G B D (capo I) "Cradle and All"

E B B F♯ B E (Martin Backpacker, capo III) "Angry Anymore"

E A D G A D "Diner," "Shameless"

D A D G A F "Hello Birmingham," "Adam and Eve"

A D A D (tenor guitar) "Little Plastic Castle," "Loom," "To the Teeth"

that I've had the money to pay people or the phone number to call when I need help of a certain sort.

In the past, you've expressed frustration with being known as the Righteous Babe CEO. Do you still feel that people have an undue awareness of you as running a business as opposed to just playing music?

DIFRANCO Yeah. That's a somewhat unique story, so I can see where the media would pick that up and run with it, and run with it, and run with it, and run with it. But after awhile, the irony of having people never actually talk about what I do, like write songs or play guitar or sing or whatever it is. . . . The people who come out to the shows know why they're there, and it's not really because of my brilliant business strategy.

Writers tend to hyphenate your music with the word punk—usually as punk-folk. But your warmth and generosity on stage is just completely out of sync with the punk attitude.

DIFRANCO Yeah, well, all of that media definition and description . . . that's why I don't read anything about me. Since the *Little Plastic Castle* record came out, I went cold turkey—I read nothing about myself, and I'm such a happier person. Because whenever you're described or defined by somebody else, you can always see what are the little pieces of you in there and what are the pieces of the person doing the talking, which can be so big sometimes.

That punk-folk hyphen business may have had to do with the kind of kinetic energy of my style, but I think it also came from people who don't know anything about the whole world of folk music, which is all about independent labels, community-based music, the DIY ethic. When they look at me, they just think, "Oh, well, punk rock do-it-yourself." That's the model a lot of people have for the DIY ethic.

I find that kind of labeling often has more to do with how somebody dresses than anything else.

DIFRANCO Yeah, right—it was probably just the shaved head, come to think of it! I try to attribute some kind of depth [*laughs*], but that's all it was, really.

It's striking how you cross generational boundaries. The audiences at your shows tend to be very young, but then you have connections with people like Greg Brown, who is baby-boomer age, and Utah Phillips . . .

DIFRANCO Long live folk music, man. When I was first poking my little badger head out of the folk music underground, I used to play to a lot of middle-aged acoustic/roots music fans. And then as word got out, there was that other contingent of young, college-aged, and then even younger listeners. It's been one of my gleeful roles to bring young people to folk festivals, and at a lot of the folk festivals that I've played in recent years there's been a really warm feeling because the people who run the thing are excited to have teenagers showing up. Of course, one of my blatantly strategic missions is to bring young audiences to people like Utah Phillips, and to Greg Brown and Gillian Welch, who I just orchestrated a tour with.

That was a dream bill, but the contrasts in style are huge. What was the common ground?

DIFRANCO Songs. It's all about the songs. Greg and I have a long-standing friendship and musical relationship, admiration from a distance kind of thing. With Gil and David, I just finally convinced them that this was a good idea, but I think they had an impression of, "Ooh, she's a rock star—I don't know what this scene is going to be like." But after the first couple of shows of starting to really hear each other's songs and play on each other's songs, we became this great musical family. It was really beautiful, and there was this atmosphere of total inspiration.

I kicked it off every night; I was kind of hostess, and I would say, "OK, the theme for the first round is . . . the song that's not finished that you're working on now." I started playing something that I was working on, and people just rose to the occasion totally.

I wanted to ask about a couple of the other people you've worked with in recent years. Bruce Cockburn, for instance: Is it true that his song "Birmingham Shadows" is about meeting you?

DIFRANCO Yes, he wrote a song about the night we met and were hanging out in Birmingham, Alabama. This crazy city festival downtown, bunch of stages. People walking around with cotton candy in the middle of the afternoon . . .

He asked me if I would do some playing or singing, just a real open-ended invitation to find my way onto his next record, and I was so busy,

WHAT THEY PLAY (2000)

Ani DiFranco carries a lot of guitar firepower on tour—currently 11 instruments, roughly eight of which are in rotation during a show. The collection includes four Alvarez-Yairi WY1s, the Bob Weir signature models that DiFranco has made her own signature. Because she attacks her guitars with a right hand bolstered by heavy plastic nails wrapped in electrical tape, she protects the beleaguered tops with an ever-expanding Batman-shaped pickguard. For deeper tones, DiFranco turns to an Alvarez AV2SB acoustic baritone (a model no longer in production) and a Danelectro electric baritone, tuned down to C. A four-string Cromwell tenor guitar gets the call for "To the Teeth" and other songs. She also picks a Martin Backpacker and two regular electrics: a Hamer and a Danelectro.

All these instruments are strung with D'Addarios: for the WY1s, she uses the EJ17 set (.013–.056), except one guitar is equipped with a .070 bass string for mega-detuning (to A, an octave below the fifth string) on the song "Dilate." The electrics get an EJ22 set (also .013–.056), while the tenor (tuned A D A D) has a surprisingly heavy .016, .024, .035, and .045 set. For capoing, she uses a Shubb.

DiFranco's main Alvarez-Yairis are amplified with Alvarez' stock System 500 pickup and preamp. The Backpacker is wired with a Fishman Matrix under-saddle pickup, and the Cromwell has a Fishman archtop pickup, which replaces the bridge. She goes wireless for the most part, through the Samson UF5D system. One of the sends coming out of the monitor console goes to a Morley Steve Vai wah pedal, the other to a volume pedal, and both plug into a little Crate VC508 amp that she overdrives on some songs. "Then we mic that," says guitar tech Reg Dickinson, "so you get a blended sound between acoustic guitar and distorted acoustic guitar, and it's a helluva sound." The electrics plug into a Rivera Sedona amp, which is miked and run direct from the effects loop.

we weren't able to make that happen. But then I just happened to be riding through New Orleans with my Goat Boy [husband] on a motorcycle, and we walked into this coffee shop and there was Bruce, sitting there. He was at Kingsway Studios, a couple blocks away, mixing his record, so he was like, "We just started mixing today. Do you want to come by and sing on this song that we're mixing?" So I just walked over and added a little harmony, but it was a very spontaneous thing.

You also have done some producing—the song "Searching for America" for Janis Ian, Dan Bern's album 50 Eggs. . . .

DIFRANCO I love to work with other people on their music, because I get all the joy of helping music to be realized without the emotional baggage of it being my own songs. It is such a blissful alternative. I'm fixing to go do some more records with other people.

Back on the subject of your music, To the Teeth *featured a lot of horn charts and sort of a sonic collision of New Orleans with the Salvation Army. Is that direction continuing?*

DIFRANCO I've always been a huge fan of brass. Actually, before I met the woman who plays keyboards with me, Julie [Wolf], I was looking for a trumpet player. I've been wanting to incorporate brass for a long time, and last summer I orchestrated this tour with Maceo Parker, where we got so tight and had so much fun playing with each other. There was no going back—I was like, "Oh, I must get my own horn section." I've been hanging a lot in New Orleans the last couple years and made a bunch of friends down there. The summer before last, I invited the Rebirth Brass Band on tour. Irvin Mayfield, the trumpeter who played on the record [on the song "Going Once"], is an incredible cat on the scene down there now.

The brass arrangements on the record are perfectly in sync with your latest songs—which, to me, are your best yet.

DIFRANCO I put so much of myself into *To the Teeth,* and I have so much love for that record, much more than I have ever felt for a record that I've made. I really felt satisfied with the work that I did there, and the relationship with my band and the people that I work with is so positive and so cool. . . . I feel like I'm just starting to hit my stride.

About the Author

Jeffrey Pepper Rodgers has been pursuing his twin passions for words and music since he was a teenager. After a stint as a freelance editor and writer for the *San Francisco Chronicle, Psychology Today,* and other publications, he became the founding editor of *Acoustic Guitar* magazine in 1990. He led the magazine through its tenth anniversary, a tenure that began with a WPA Maggie Award for Best New Consumer Magazine and ended with *Acoustic Guitar* as one of two finalists in the entertainment category of the Folio: Editorial Excellence Awards. At the same time he wrote scores of articles and helped to launch new ventures into books, CD compilations, the Web, and other areas. These days he continues to write extensively for the magazine, and he is the editor for String Letter Publishing's book division. His writing has also appeared in *The Joni Mitchell Companion* (Schirmer), Dave Matthews and Tim Reynolds' *Live at Luther College* songbook (Cherry Lane), and the guidebooks *Performing Acoustic Music* and *Songwriting and the Guitar* (String Letter Publishing).

As a musician, Rodgers has been writing and playing original songs for more than 20 years, and he has performed in San Francisco Bay Area clubs with his brother, Andy, and their quartet, Heavy Wood. His all-acoustic, home-recorded CD, *Traveling Songs,* can be sampled at www.JeffreyPepperRodgers.com, along with some of his writings about music and other subjects. In addition to singing and playing the guitar, Rodgers has studied North Indian tabla drumming extensively, both in the U.S. and in India.

OTHER TITLES IN THE BACKSTAGE BOOKS SERIES

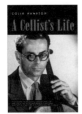

A Cellist's Life, by Colin Hampton, $12.95
One of the 20th century's most distinguished cellists, Colin Hampton is your guide to a bygone world of classical music and musicians. Through his witty, convivial, and candid narrative, you'll encounter such luminaries as Pablo Casals, Ernest Bloch, Igor Stravinsky, Arturo Toscanini, Béla Bartók, and Yehudi Menuhin.

21st-Century Violinists, Vol. 1, $12.95
An exciting collection of in-depth inverviews with the world's preeminent string players, including Corey Cerovsek, Sarah Chang, Pamela Frank, Kennedy, Midori, Anne-Sophie Mutter, Elmar Oliveira, Nadja Salerno-Sonnenberg, Gil Shaham, Isaac Stern, and Maxim Vengerov.

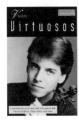

Violin Virtuosos, $12.95
This fascinating companion to Vol. 1 includes profiles of Joshua Bell, Chee-Yun, Kyung-Wha Chung, Jorja Fleezanis, Hilary Hahn, Leila Josefowicz, Mark Kaplan, Viktoria Mullova, Vadim Repin, Joseph Silverstein, and Christian Tetzlaff.

21st-Century String Quartets, Vol. 1, $12.95
In this collection of in-depth interviews, today's leading performers get to the heart of one of the most beloved forms of classical music: the string quartet. You are backstage with the American, Borodin, Emerson, Guarneri, Juilliard, Mandelring, Manhattan, Mendelssohn, Orion, St. Petersburg, and Tokyo String Quartets.

For more information on books from String Letter Publishing, or to place an order, please call Music Dispatch at (800) 637-2852, fax (414) 774-3259, or mail to Music Dispatch, PO Box 13920, Milwaukee, WI 53213. Visit String Letter Publishing on-line at www.stringletter.com.